How to Succeed as an Entrepreneur in Africa
A Practical Guide and Cases

Adonis & Abbey Publishers Ltd and mRAN publications

St James House
24 Old Queen Street,
London SW1H 9HP
United Kingdom

Website: http://www.adonis-abbey.com
E-mail Address: editor@adonis-abbey.com

Nigeria:
Suites C4 – C6 J-Plus Plaza
Asokoro, Abuja, Nigeria
Tel: +234 (0) 7058078841/08052035034

British Library Cataloguing-in-Publication Data
A catalogue record for this book is available from the British Library

ISBN: 978-1-913976-08-8

How to Succeed as an Entrepreneur in Africa
A Practical Guide and Cases

John Kuada and Madei Mangori

Table of Contents

Acknowledgements...vi

Part 1

Chapter One
Mindset as the First Key to Business Success 9

Chapter Two
Making Profits for a Purpose. 19

Chapter Three
Growing Businesses..27

Chapter Four
Designing a Winning Strategy..37

Chapter Five
Managing Efficiently and Effectively...43

Chapter Six
Developing and Maintaining Trust with Business Partners 49

Chapter Seven
Managing Employees Well 53

Chapter Eight
Choosing an Appropriate Leadership Style 57

Chapter Nine
Communicating with Maturity..65

Chapter Ten
Engaging in Fast Learning..71

Chapter Eleven
Generating and Sustaining Positive Human Energy..................................75

Chapter Twelve
Managing Time Effectively 81

Chapter Thirteen
Putting Customers at the Centre of Management Decisions 84

Chapter Fourteen
Financial Health Assessment 91

Part 2: Profiles of Successful African Entrepreneurs

1. The Story of Mr Thatayaone Dichaba
2. The Story of Mr Peter Cunningham
3. The Story of Dr Collen Msasanure
4. The Story of Mr Davidson Norupiri
5. The Story of Mr Chenjerai Tsuro
6. The Story of Mrs Edna Mukurazhizha
7. The Story of Ms Wendy Luhabe
8. Reflections on the Profiles

Part 3: Case Studies

1. Farmer Business (Pty) Ltd
2. Shareholder Growth Sustenance (Pty) Ltd
3. Waste Management Pro (Pty) Ltd
4. Botho Country Lodge (BCL) (Pty) Ltd
5. ProductionPro (Pty) Ltd

Bibliography 154

Index 157

Acknowledgements

The motivation for writing this book came mainly from owners of small businesses in Botswana, Ghana, South Africa and Zimbabwe who had spoken with us during management training sessions and workshops in the past three decades. They have repeatedly drawn our attention to the lack of practical guidelines that will help new business owners improve the performance of their companies and remain confident and determined in the face of adversities. This is a daunting task and this book is an initial response to this appeal. The book seeks to provide African entrepreneurs with some suggestions and pointers at sources of solutions to the challenges that they are likely to face. We are grateful to all the managers whose experiences have provided us with inspiration and insights into the way businesses are run in Africa.

Part 1

CHAPTER ONE

Mindset as the First Key to Business Success

Introduction

Successful people are keenly aware that no human being can have everything s/he wants. However, everyone can have what really matters to them if they work really hard for a really long period of time. We all have the potential within us to be an achiever. The starting point is the determination within us to nurture our potentials and to bring about real change. When the determination is there, everything else begins to move in the direction that we desire. The moment one resolves to be an achiever, every nerve and fibre within one's body immediately orients itself towards success. The desire to start a business may be driven by such a determination – the determination to make a difference rather than barely survive. Most business people see achievement as more important than material or financial reward. Achievement gives them greater personal satisfaction than receiving praise or recognition. They regard financial reward as a measurement of success, not an end in itself.

This book is intended for those business-owners who cultivate such an inner desire to grow their businesses and to use the results of their efforts to make a real difference in their own lives and those of hundreds or even thousands of people within and outside Africa. It narrates stories of those Africans that have successfully grown their businesses and have made notable contributions to society as business people. It also provides guidelines that can help them succeed and offers insights into some of the challenges that they are likely to face.

Agambire and Agams Holding Company[1]

Let us start with the story of Mr Roland Agambire, one of Ghana's celebrated entrepreneurs of today. Mr Agambire, who describes himself as a born entrepreneur, has been described by some journalists as a personification of determination. His story started as that of any other Ghanaian "village boy". Born in Sirigu, a farming community in northern Ghana, as one of about 50 children to a father with 10 wives, his background and challenges in early childhood became a source of determination for him to turn his life around. However, he hardly expected the achievement that he has been able to record before turning 40. As a child, he slept beside 10 of his siblings on the same mat, "like prisoners in a crowded jail", he recalls. His entrepreneurial talent manifested itself before he turned 10. He noticed that, when the older men got drunk, they became careless with their money, dropping some of the coins in their pockets. The young Roland, therefore, decided to make the collection of coins his business. He went from one drinking spot to the other, looking for coins that might have fallen out of the pockets of the customers. This enabled him to "earn" his own pocket money while going to school. His next move was to use his savings to start producing and selling snacks to his school mates. This quickly turned into trading in essential household items such as kerosene. Since his village was close to the Burkina Faso border, he decided to cross the border with kerosene and cigarettes – items that were in a shorter supply in the border towns. This was the beginning of his export business. By the mid-1990s, his trading activities had expanded and he dabbled in cash crops exportation.

Today, Roland Agambire is the CEO of Agams Holdings comprising 11 integrated companies. He is also the Chairman and CEO of Rlg Communications Group (a leading ICT company), employing more than 500 permanent staff and 10,000 casual workers with an annual turnover of about two billion US dollars. Agams Holdings has interests in oil, construction, computing and telecommunications, financial services, and

---

[1] Information presented in the book about Agambire and Agams Holdings is from various Internet Sources. See https://en.wikipedia.org/wiki/Roland_Agambire; http://www.rlgglobal.c om/AGAMS-Holdings; http://eataghana.com/2016/08/13/biography-of-roland-agambire-ceo-of-rlg-and-agams-holdings; http://www.marcopolis.net/agams-holdings-building-a-legacy-in-african-ict-sector.htm - All retrieved on January 9, 2017

trading. In 2012, Agambire's Rlg was ranked the second best company in Ghana by the Ghana Investment Promotion Centre. In January 2013, the Pan African Television Network, E-TV, voted him "the Most Influential Ghanaian for the year 2012" in a poll it conducted among its viewers. He was also voted "the Entrepreneur of the Year 2012" in a competition organised by the Entrepreneur Foundation of Ghana.

How can we explain Mr. Agambire's extraordinary achievement? The starting point of all human achievements is the type of mindset one cultivates as one grows into adulthood. In her book *Mindset: The New Psychology of Success*, Stanford psychologist Carol Dweck (2006) informs us that our views about our own abilities and potential (both conscious and unconscious) fuel our behaviour in life and predict our success. She argues that some people are guided overwhelmingly by a *fixed mindset*. A fixed mindset assumes that our character, intelligence and creative ability are static givens which we cannot change in any meaningful way. In contrast, some people seem to have a *growth mindset*. This *growth mindset* is based on the belief that our basic qualities can be cultivated through our own efforts. This means those with a growth mindset will thrive on challenges and will experience failure as a springboard for growth.

Mr Agambire cultivated a growth mindset from early childhood. As a child, he strongly felt that he deserved a lot more in life than his family background appeared to have dictated, and he was determined not to be a slave to his destiny. As the American writer Debbie Millman states, *"if you imagine less, less will be what you undoubtedly deserve"*. The determination to change one's destiny provides the inner motivation to live one's life with curiosity and a high level of attentiveness as one goes through life. These are important personality traits that successful entrepreneurs exhibit. Successful business people are, therefore, described as people with a strong desire for autonomy, independence, creativity and tolerance of ambiguity, moderately risk-loving, and the determination to win. Societies that emphasise these attributes in the upbringing of their children will have many young people turn out to be entrepreneurs. It has also been noted that formal education may not be necessary for starting a new business. Many high school and college dropouts have become successful entrepreneurs throughout history.

Building on the above understanding, one can argue that the African culture is not always helpful in nurturing entrepreneurial talents. For example, a Ghanaian sociologist, Professor Assimeng (1981), describes the Ghanaian personality as characterised by:

1. conformity and blatant eschewing of individual speculations;
2. unquestioning acquiescence;
3. lack of self-reliance, owing to the pervading influence of the extended family system;
4. fetish worship of authority and charismatic leaders; and
5. hatred for criticism.

These characteristics may be found in other African societies and clearly constrain individual initiatives and entrepreneurial zeal. Seen against this background, Mr Agambire's achievements are extraordinary and an indication of the strength of his personality. Naturally, he has been described as a man of action. Most successful entrepreneurs agree that comfort is a major constraint to success. Business owners need to strive always to go beyond their comfort zone in order to be successful in any endeavour in life. Seeking comfort leads to an acceptance of mediocre performance. One may not be the smartest person in Africa. However, that does not matter. If an individual multiplies all his actions by 10, he will definitely out-compete all others within his line of business. Once a person gets moving, one rides with the momentum. Consistent action allows entrepreneurs to gain knowledge and experiences fast.

One of the latest additions to Mr Agambire's blossoming empire is the Hope City project, which is estimated to be something in the region of US$10 billion. The Hope City, when completed, will have provided offices, accommodation for more than 50,000 people and will also host some of the tallest buildings on the continent. This is not going to be the end. Mr Agambire has also taken actions in other fields of endeavour. Despite his business success, he has been eager to study. He has taken courses in export and marketing offered by the Ghana Export Promotion Council. He has also completed a bachelor's degree in business administration at the Ghana Institute of Management and Public Administration (GIMPA).

Mr Agambire was reported to tell the American business magazine, *Forbes*, that poverty is a perception. "It is the mind that changes the human being,"[2] he observed. Thus, regardless of how small one's beginning might be, with hard work and the right thinking, one would

[2] See http://www.modernghana.com/news/490266/1/rlgs-roland-agambire-an-inspiration-to-ghanaian-yo.html

end up being what one always envisages being," he added. It is important to bear in mind that poverty is more than just a lack of income. It also connotes lack of respect, self-worth, dignity, inclusion, choice and security. Poverty makes people resign to their living conditions and holds their creativity in check. Thus, poverty sets a negative spiral in motion. This means any effort made to alleviate poverty is itself growth-propelling since it unleashes hitherto untapped psychological and physical human resources within a community and thereby helps transform a negative spiral into a positive one. Poverty alleviation is, therefore, not a philanthropic project but a viable business proposition.

Having an Attentive Mindset

Most writers suggest that the entrepreneurial process starts with the "discovery" of opportunities. The discovery is usually done by alert individuals who are at all times scanning the horizon, as it were, ready to make discoveries. If we look closely into the Ghanaian economy today, there are numerous opportunities to do business and the very attentive individuals identify these opportunities and exploit them – some successfully. This is also true for many other African countries. All economic analysts agree that there is a growing middle income group in nearly all African countries. Out of the 54 countries, 24 of them more than doubled their per capita income over 1990-2010. Household spending in Africa is projected to increase from $860 billion in 2008 to $1.4 trillion in 2020 (McKinsey, 2010). Furthermore, Africa's population is likely to grow to two billion people and account for 20 % of the world's population by 2050. As a whole, African consumers have remained underserved and underserviced and are waiting for attentive and hard-working business owners to serve them.

Psychologists have always reminded us that paying attention is a disciplined art. It requires taking the time to observe from a variety of perspectives. Attentive individuals are able to discern the unfamiliar in the familiar, as well as the familiar in the unfamiliar.

Once again, Mr Roland Agambire's story illustrates this quite well. RLG had a modest beginning as a company. It started as Roagam Links in March 2001, repairing mobile phones, thereby serving the emerging needs of urban Ghanaians most of whom had acquired mobile phones for the first time. After successfully increasing RLG's market share by repairing mobile phones, the company began manufacturing them in 2008. Today, RLG assembles laptop computers, tablets, electronic notebooks, LCD television monitors, mobile handsets and various other types of communications equipment. In collaboration with Ghana's Ministry of Youth and Sports, RLG has established a training programme that aims to teach ICT-related disciplines to 30,000 young Ghanaians.

> *"The range of what we think and do is limited by what we fail to notice. And because we fail to notice that we fail to notice, there is little we can do to change; until we notice how failing to notice shapes our thoughts and deeds." – R. D. Laing*
>
> *See https://www.brainyquote.com/quotes/quotes/r/rdlaing130951.html*

Mr Agambire sees himself as a visionary Ghanaian entrepreneur. He was quick to realise that Ghana needed to introduce its youths to the intricacies of ICT and train them to take advantage of its economic potential. As he explains,

> I had a vision regarding the potential of developing ICT in Africa……….. It is not just about touching a computer and printing a document. The devices, the software and the overall supporting technology offer vast opportunities, and young Africans are starting to understand the possibilities behind these technologies.

Reflecting on the evolution of RLG, Mr Agambire noted in an interview that "the perception of the people was a key determinant in the company's success". He has encouraged his staff to be observant and take notes of how consumers respond to their products and service offerings. He explained: "We had to show Ghanaian people that our products were not just local. They are certified to international standards, and when people use an RLG product, the way it feels and responds is no different from that of renowned products from the United States or Europe."

Cultivate a Fighting Spirit

The achiever mindset builds a tenacity of character. Commitment and tenacity enable people to try something bold. Conventional wisdom teaches us that anything worth having is worth striving for with all one's might. It is also often said that, if one succeeds in everything one does, then one is probably not pushing oneself hard enough. People who push themselves may risk failure when they do so. One learns nothing of value if one does not fail or knows how to handle failures.

> *"Every great success has always been achieved by fight. Every winner has scars....The men who succeed are the efficient few. They are the few who have the ambition and will-power to develop themselves. So choose to be among the few today."*
>
> *– Chris Kirubi - a Kenyan entrepreneur*

Successful entrepreneurs need to learn to manage their failures. The owner and executive director of another well-known Ghanaian company, Nana Owusu-Afari of the Afariwaa Group of Companies, knows this well. He started his entrepreneurial journey in 1970, as "hobby" poultry farmer. The poultry farm was located in his backyard, in Tema. The success he enjoyed from the farm encouraged him to quit his job in 1976 and to move the farm onto a leased parcel of farmland from the Tema Development Corporation. He was willing to sacrifice the comfort that regular incomes provide and accept the uncertainties that start-ups bring with them. Today, the Afariwaa Group of Companies has varied interests in farming, real estate development, veterinary pharmaceuticals, bottled water processing and production. It also has substantial shareholding in a couple of local banks. In a recent interview, Nana Owusu-Afari reflected on this journey and said:

> The path to success, as a private sector operator, has not always been easy. It takes grit, a healthy sense of self-confidence, and an equally healthy dose of nationalistic fervour to traverse the turbulent and rough terrain of growing a business from start-up, through early stages of

growth to a well-established business that is capable of surviving on its own strength

It is also often said that 'adversity is a blessing in disguise'. Every failure teaches the successful individual what must be avoided in the future. It also develops fortitude and courage. To John Maxwell the author of the *Failing Forward*, "the difference between average people and achieving people is their perception of and response to failure". To him, failure is simply a price we pay to achieve success. Thus, when achievers fail, they see it as a momentary event, not a lifelong epidemic. His argument is that how people see failure and deal with it impacts every aspect of their lives. He, therefore, urges every person to learn to "fail forward". That is, we must accept failure as part of progress, challenge outdated assumptions that guide our actions, take new risks and persevere, irrespective of previous negative outcomes.

- *Embrace adversity and make failure a regular part of your life. If you're not failing, you're probably not really moving forward.*

- *The next time you find yourself envying what successful people have achieved, recognise that they have probably gone through many negative experiences that you cannot see on the surface.*

  — John Maxwell (Author of *Failing Forward*)

John Maxwell suggests that there are seven key abilities that allow people to take each setback in life as a springboard to success. We can take an inspiration from these as a good starting point in our discussions of how to succeed as an entrepreneur in Africa. The seven abilities are as follows:

1. **Reject rejection.** He argues that successful people do not blame themselves when they fail. They take responsibility for each setback, but they do not take the failure personally.
2. **View failure as temporary.** Rejection of failure means, in effect, that when people fail, they view their failures as temporary, that is, they do not personalise their failures or see their problems as holes they are permanently stuck in.
3. **View each failure as an isolated incident.** Seeing each failure as a temporary (rather than permanent) condition of life also means that each setback is just a small part of the whole and an opportunity to learn what not to do.
4. **Have realistic expectations.** High achievers are constantly aware that success takes time. In other words, there are going to be bumps along the way when one aims at something worthwhile.
5. **Focus on strengths.** Experience has shown that high achievers focusing on leveraging and amplifying their strengths rather feel constrained by their weaknesses. The focus on strengths rather than weaknesses allows people to multiply their results.
6. **Vary approaches.** Achievers explore alternative solutions to every challenge they face and select what appears to them to be the most appropriate under given circumstances. However, they are willing to vary their approaches to the problems they face. They do not repose a blind faith in any given approach. Maxwell advises that if one's approach appears not working and brings repeated failures, then one must try something else. The understanding here is that what works for one person may not necessarily work for another.
7. **Bounce back.** Finally, successful people are resilient. They do not let one error keep them down. They learn from their mistakes and move on.

CHAPTER TWO

Making Profits for a Purpose

Introduction

It is important for business owners to think about the type of entrepreneurs they want to be and the vision for their businesses. Some of them may see their businesses as "survival workshops", that is, they engage in business out of sheer necessity. They would have loved to be salaried employees if they had the opportunity to get jobs. Their businesses, therefore, become temporary occupations or sources of refuge. Others may be fortunate to have salaried jobs and see their businesses as sources of supplementary incomes. Those who fall into one of these two categories are not likely to look for opportunities to grow their businesses. However, some owners may see the businesses as fetching more income than initially expected and, therefore, begin to devote increasing amounts of time and resources to them. Their visions for the businesses will then change, and they will be willing to consider growth strategies.

Those who are not survival entrepreneurs may have higher goals for their business endeavours right from the beginning. They may reflect on the following questions: What should be the overriding vision of my business? If I want to be rich, what value do I aim at creating with my wealth? This chapter provides business owners with some ideas to help them reflect on these issues and take a stand that will guide their visions and missions for their businesses.

The Meaning in Life and Business

David W. Johnson the author of *Reaching Out* reminds us that life is characterised by an ongoing search for both daily bread and daily meaning. The primary determinant of meaning in life is other people. Our lives are shaped by the relationships we share with others and the relationships of thousands of other people. Human beings are, therefore, described as social animals. For many people, living purposefully means staying focused not only on what is important for oneself but also on what creates value and makes life meaningful for others. This is also true for business ventures. Business performances are, therefore, no longer measured only in terms of profit. Elkington (2004) coined the term 'Triple Bottom Line' (TLP) to draw attention to the higher goals of businesses. The triple bottom line are reflected in the 3Ps (profit, people and planet). The performance of businesses must be concurrently assessed in terms of the impact of their operations on people within and outside the companies as well as the planet in general. In other words, companies must earn profits, because such profits are essential for further business growth and even survival. However, earned profits should be reasonable, just, and not earned at the cost of various other stakeholders, especially the community or the environment. Furthermore, companies operate through the actions of employees and provide their products and services to other people. As such, it is the responsibility of businesses to safeguard the interests of all persons that they relate directly to, i.e. within and outside the companies.

> *"From the standpoint of daily life, there is one thing we do know: that we are here for the sake of each other - above all for those upon whose smile and well-being our own happiness depends, and also for the countless unknown souls with whose fate we are connected by a bond of sympathy. Many times a day I realise how much my own outer and inner life is built upon the labours of my fellow men, both living and dead, and how earnestly I must exert myself in order to give in return as much as I have received."*
>
> *- Albert Einstein*

The world is now seeing the rise of a new kind of entrepreneur, who is determined to address the world's most pressing needs through business activities. These entrepreneurs tend to believe that they have an incredible opportunity to use their businesses as forces for good and make a tremendous difference in the world. They want to make profit for a purpose.

Even those who have been pushed into business out of sheer necessity still have the potential to grow their businesses. As Steven Covey (the author of *The 7 Habits of Highly Effective People*) encourages us, "no matter how long we've walked life's pathway to mediocrity, we can always choose to switch paths". This means we all have the power to decide to live a *great* life, – a life of an outstanding businessperson in

Africa. Thus, it is no longer enough for a businessperson to figure out how to make a profit. Money is still important, but business owners must not consider money as the be-all and end-all of business. They must see money as a tool to achieving another end, i.e. to fulfil a purpose. This means they must make profit for a purpose. They must use the money they earn to fulfil their dreams of impacting the world. This may take the form of creating new job opportunities or helping other businesses to grow so that the communities in which they live prosper. Entrepreneurs that pursue social motives as integral parts of their businesses are also referred to as humanitarian or social entrepreneurs. They combine two fantastic and motivating aspects of business undertakings – the ability to do business and the ability to create social values. In other words, they turn corporate social responsibility into their core business.

Some of business owners may be good at identifying business opportunities and providing innovative solutions to problems within their environments and, therefore, create viable business ventures out of these endeavours. Those who do so may also be growth-oriented. Growth-oriented entrepreneurs are usually described as those who can combine a strong desire for growth with the potential capacity to realise it.

Serving the Poor for Profit and Purpose

It is crucial to emphasise that businesses can and should not only create economic value, but also engage constructively with the community where they are located. Some business owners may not get rich quickly but they will enjoy the satisfaction that social contributions provide. Furthermore, it is not always necessary for entrepreneurs to have a crystal clear vision of who they are; what they want to do; and where they want to go before they start. It is enough to be guided by faith in the simple truth that they are in this world to be of value to mankind. As Dr Martin Luther King Jr. says, "take the first step in faith. You don't have to see the whole staircase. Just take the first step". This is a view adopted by most religious entrepreneurs. They believe that God (The Universe, Source, etc.) gave them unique talents and gifts for a specific reason. They are destined to create and serve others.

> *"Be the change that you wish to see in the world"*
>
> *– Mahatma Gandhi*

It is becoming evident in both developed world and the developing world that great companies are not great just because they make lots of money. They make lots of money precisely because they are great. In Africa, the conventional marketing logic tends to consider many Africans as being too poor to be viable customers. Prahalad (2005) has a different perspective. He estimates that the poor people of the world have buying power equal to $8 billion per day. This makes the poor a multitrillion-dollar annual market on a global scale. Considering the fact that the African population is growing rapidly and is expected to be two billion within the next three decades, businesses can hardly afford to ignore even the poor segments of the population. Kotler and Lee (2009) convey the same perception when they argue that the poor have the right to want what the rich want and, as a group, they constitute an incipient demand waiting to be tapped.

Fred Swaniker

Some successful Ghanaian business owners are beginning to see the wisdom in this approach to business. They are keenly aware that it is not possible to do long-lasting business in this country without contributing in some significant manner to society. They see themselves as part of their social contexts, for better or for worse.

One of these types of young Ghanaian entrepreneurs is Fred Swaniker (born in 1976) to a Ghanaian magistrate (father) and educationist (mother). Before he turned 30, he had lived in four African countries (Ghana, Gambia, Botswana and Zimbabwe), attended Macalester College in Minnesota as well as Stanford School of Business (USA), worked for McKinsey & Company in South Africa, and established African Leadership Academy, African Leadership Network, Global Leadership Adventures and Africa Advisory Group. He was praised by Barack Obama and other prominent leaders for his entrepreneurial achievements. His motivation to start African Leadership Academy came from his reflections on the situation that wealthy African families send their children to the US and UK for good university education. He wondered why Africa could not establish a top-notch school for African students in Africa. Drawing on his Silicon Valley connections, he was able to raise funds to establish the Academy in 2004. In 2016, he opened the doors to his latest entrepreneurial ventures – The African Leadership University – in partnership with Scotland's Glasgow Caledonian University. The University's overriding goal is to train high-calibre leaders who will drive Africa's development and inspire generations to come. The University is currently located in Mauritius with the ambition of building 25 campuses across the continent and training three million leaders in five decades.

Robert Asare

Entrepreneurial visions do not emerge fully formed overnight from the entrepreneur's head, but rather evolve over a span of time, following a period of exploration, talking to people, reading, reflecting, etc. Another prominent Ghanaian entrepreneur that demonstrates the "profit for purpose" orientation to entrepreneurship is Mr Robert Asare, the owner of Ghana Craft Company (name changed to preserve its anonymity). The idea of establishing Ghana Craft Company (GCC) was hatched in the mid-1980s when Robert Asare was then the CEO of the Ghanaian subsidiary of a major European company. He had always considered Ghanaian handicrafts to have distinctive features and, therefore, brought them as gifts for his European and North American friends on his business trips. For many years, he had wondered why the sector had not grown into a viable industry that contributed substantially to economic growth and poverty alleviation in the country. For most artisans, the production of handicraft products had remained a hobby rather than a source of significant and sustainable income. This meant that they hardly showed commitment to their work and lacked motivation to upgrade their skills, let alone introduce new products. He believed he could help transform the sector through the use of his professional experience and business contacts.

In 1988, Robert Asare asked the marketing director of his former company, James Banor (who had also retired), to join him in building GCC into a strong intermediary for the handicraft sector. He and Banor subsequently conducted some preliminary investigations to uncover the domestic and export opportunities for the best known handicraft products in the country. The information they gathered suggested that the economic policies initiated by the Ghanaian government in the mid-1980s were making positive contributions to the industry's growth. By the late 1980s, Ghana was acclaimed by the World Bank and other international economic monitors to be at the threshold of economic lift-off. There were increasing numbers of foreign visitors in the country, creating a healthy market for handicrafts. They reasoned that if the products were sold in convenient locations and were appropriately packaged, tourists visiting Ghana would be willing to pay higher prices for them and this would help grow the sector. Asare and Banor consequently opened souvenir shops close to major shopping centres in Accra, Tema and Kumasi. They reasoned further that the tourists would serve as windows to the export markets since their buying behaviour would be indicative of the preferences of potential consumers in the major European and North American countries.

The handicraft industry in Ghana grew from these modest beginnings. In the 1990s, the industry was estimated to be worth barely US$200, 000 in annual sales. This grew to a US$28-million industry by 2011. An estimated number of 50, 000 handicraft producers now depend fully or partly on the sector for their livelihoods, and 5, 000 of them produce for the export market.

In 2005, a comprehensive training programme was initiated, aimed at upgrading the production skills of the local artisans and raising their awareness of hazardous production methods. About 2% of its earnings have been redistributed among the rural-based producers in the form of bonuses and provision of raw materials. Another 2% are now spent on corporate social investments such as construction of school buildings and provision of other facilities to the primary schools in the major handicraft production regions.

The company has also established two "enhanced handicraft production centres" in Accra and Tamale to serve artisans in the southern and northern parts of Ghana, respectively. The centres are manned by six well-trained "master artisans" – three at each centre. Products bought from artisans in the rural areas were brought to the centre where the master artisans supervised younger apprentices to provide them with neater finishing touches before they were shipped to the market. The centres also provided training at substantially subsidised costs to local artisans that would like to improve their skills.

The Challenges of Socially Responsible Entrepreneurship

The "profit for purpose" vision may be a challenge for some of people due to the African culture and the obligations imposed by our extended family systems. Business scholars who have studied the growth ambitions of African entrepreneurs tend to agree that African family systems can sometimes be a drag on our economic efforts. African business owners are expected to spend their earnings on kinship obligations such as financing the studies of brothers, cousins, nephews and nieces; lodging newcomers (from rural areas arriving in the major towns to escape poverty); and financing the multitude of ceremonies that fill the African social life.

One of the authors of this book has discussed this issue at length with a number of Ghanaian entrepreneurs during the past three decades. Nearly all of them agree to the cultural constraints of succeeding as an entrepreneur in Ghana. One of the business owners who has commented on the issue is the owner of Environmental Development Group (EDG), which started on a very small scale in Ho in the Volta Region. When he established his first business (a bakery) in the 1970s, he had to give it up due to conflicts with his cousin. When he started his second business, his dad asked him to employ some of his relatives, although they did not have the required business skills and experience. However, once they were employed, it became extremely difficult to fire them, even those who were caught using business assets for their own personal purposes. The older relatives depended on him several years after their retirement, even after he had paid them their gratuity and other entitlements. "But what else can I do?" he asked, inviting the interviewer's understanding during the discussions. He explained the situation further:

> Our Ghanaian culture has inbuilt taken-for-granted birth-rights for family members. Many assume that it is their birth-right to have a share of the wealth of the relatively better-off members of their families without giving anything in return…. As a person, I am soft by nature. This makes it difficult for me to reconcile the needs of my business with the expectations of family members.

Some entrepreneurs have sought to address this problem in a creative (but unorthodox) manner. They simply decide to "de-link" themselves from the family while their businesses are young. Those entrepreneurs who deliberately disconnected themselves from their families came back to the family fold when their businesses had gained a stronger economic foundation and could withstand the predatory tendencies of their families. There may be some lessons to learn from these entrepreneurs.

CHAPTER THREE

Growing Businesses

Introduction

Starting a new business is usually a decision that comes with excitement. However, growing a business is another story. It is often said that being an entrepreneur is a marathon activity with lots of sprints. Entrepreneurs may need to win a lot of little races, and this will provide them and their employees with momentum. Issues of prioritisation of business owners' resources, including time, are important. How do they gain attention for themselves and their companies – make their companies known and significant? How do they gain more customers? How do they make sure that customers become loyal to their companies? They will continue to grapple with these questions for many years in their business life. This chapter provides some tips on how to stay on the growth path right from the beginning of an entrepreneurial journey.

Be Focused

Entrepreneurs must focus their time, energy and financial resources in order to succeed. They need to avoid establishing several small businesses that are run concurrently. Although business owners may think that they can reduce their risks of business collapsing by diversifying their investments and income base, such a diversification at an early stage of their business life may become sources of setbacks. Spreading their capital and managerial time over many small activities means that none of these businesses receives the attention and resources it deserves in order to grow or survive during difficult times.

Some entrepreneurs may be good at identifying business opportunities and providing innovative solutions to problems within their environment and, therefore, create viable business ventures out of these endeavours. These types of entrepreneurs are termed as being growth-oriented. They are able to combine a strong desire for growth with the potential capacity to realise it. Most writers on entrepreneurship agree that the attributes that characterise growth-oriented entrepreneurs include tenacity, perseverance, persistency, determination, commitment, resilience, self-confidence, adaptability, flexibility, networking abilities and passion. These are coupled with an understanding of the needs of the market and the goods and services one seeks to offer. Certainly not all successful entrepreneurs have all these attributes from the beginning of their entrepreneurial journey. Most people develop them as they gain experience with their business ventures.

Be Quick at Spotting Opportunities

To be a growth-oriented entrepreneur, one needs to be able to recognise an opportunity within the business environment. Specifically, one needs to be able to identify a problem or gap, and come up with an innovative solution. A popular anecdote frequently told to students at international business workshops goes like this: The management of a footwear company sent one of their salespersons to an African town. When he got there, he immediately wrote back to his manager: "There is no market for our products here – no one uses footwear here." A competitor to the first company sent its salesperson to the same town. He, in turn, wrote back to his manager, "send a truck load of sandals – no one uses footwear here." This anecdote illustrates very well how two persons can perceive the same business environment differently.

The same idea holds true in most African countries. A quick look at the business environment will show that there are business opportunities all around. The question is to know where to look. Let us take one example. The domestic market for fruit juices has been growing strongly in recent years, in part, because African consumers are showing increasing appreciation for the natural taste and health benefits of agricultural products in Africa. In Ghana for example, it has been estimated that 10.4 million litres of fruit juice are consumed yearly. However, approximately 70% of the juice products are imported, although Ghana is endowed with an assortment of fruits, including mangoes, pineapples, citrus and coconut, among others. Furthermore, the country's location offers conditions that are close to optimum for growing tropical fruits. The opportunity to transform agricultural produce into juice and other value added consumer products for domestic and foreign markets and ultimately dominate the processed fruits industry exists, but few local companies have taken advantage of this opportunity.

The story of Danso Fruit Drinks (named changed to preserve anonymity) provides a good illustration of how some successful Ghanaian entrepreneurs capture opportunities (Tesar and Kuada, 2013). It was the first registered Ghanaian company to produce tropical fruit juice. It all started when the founder (Mr Charles Danso) attended an enterprise development seminar in 1985. The seminar entirely changed the direction of his life. One of the speakers at the seminar talked about the local fruit production and marketing system in Ghana at that time. He informed the participants that fruits and vegetables produced in Ghana were harvest-dependent seasonal products, available only during certain periods of the year, and had a limited storage life. Thus, the domestic market was usually glutted during the harvest season – prices were low and the post-harvest losses were very high. Consumers hardly got fresh fruits to buy for the rest of the year, and those which reached the market were sold at extremely high prices. Thus, year-round fruit consumption was a luxury that only the relatively rich consumers could afford. In his view, one of the supply-related challenges faced by the sector was to design a production system that could ensure a year-round production. Furthermore, the local fruit-processing industry was under-developed with only a handful of small-scale processing activities. Large volume fruit processing for the mass market did not exist. There was, therefore, a marketing gap that needed to be filled.

After the seminar, Mr Danso became obsessed with the idea of creating his own business, and it should be in the fruit-processing industry. He decided to retire from his position as a bank manager. He was at the time in his early fifties. With all his children in their early 20s, he felt he could venture into new spheres of life with the uncertainties that come with entrepreneurial ventures.

The first challenge, in his view, was to set up a fruit-processing facility of a significant size and to find someone knowledgeable in fruits processing to handle the production. He would also need to organise the purchasing, transportation and storage of fruits during the harvest seasons. He discussed his ideas with his uncle, Mr Alfred Amanea, a chemistry lecturer from the University of Ghana who had some working experience from the Ghana Standards Board (GSB). They agreed to establish the business together. They also agreed that it would be wise for the company to establish its own farms in order to reduce its dependence on the local fruit farmers, since there were no recognised commercial fruit farms in the country at that time. This would help ensure a year-round supply of the fruits for the processing factory.

The company was established in 1987 and was named Danso Fruit Drinks (DFD). Danso was the name of a popular TV evangelist in Ghana at that time. Although Mr Danso did not have any family relationship with the preacher, taking on the name provided the company and its products with unaided and instantaneous brand identification. However, it conveyed an association of ethical probity.

Thus, DFD became a front-runner company in the cultivation, processing and marketing of tropical fruit juice in Ghana. By 1995, the company had 5000 hectares of pineapple, 1000 hectares of orange and 300 hectares of mangoes under cultivation. Mr Danso became the majority shareholder with 60% of the equity. His uncle's contribution was 30% of the equity, while Mr Danso's wife, Catherine, bought 10% equity. In 2003, the company's farms had been expanded to 7000 hectares of pineapples, 5000 hectares of oranges, 2000 hectares of mangoes, 1000 hectares of papaya in addition to guava, passion fruit and a few other exotic tropical fruits cultivated on an experimental basis.

DFD started production of a small batch of pineapple juice in 1989. The product was sold in 1 litre Tetra Pak containers, mainly to the catering sector and to hotels in Accra. In 1992, it added mango and orange juice to its products. By 2003, the variety of tropical fruit juices produced by the company had increased to include papaya, guava, citrus and various combinations of these fruits into different types of juices. Sales began to grow rapidly from 1995 when the company began to sell its products to the broader market segment in 200 ml Tetra Pak containers and changed its distribution system to serve this market segment.

> *"History has demonstrated that the most notable winners usually encountered heartbreaking obstacles before they triumphed. They won because they refused to become discouraged by their defeats."*
>
> – B.C. Forbes

Turn Problems into Opportunities

Going back to the mindset discussion in chapter one, it is important to stress once again that our mindset is a key determinant of how we see the world. It is often said that how we think about a problem is more important than the problem itself. In the same vein, Albert Einstein argues that the significant problems we face in life cannot be solved at the same level of thinking we were when we created them. These perspectives on solving problems in daily life apply to business as well. Too often, we focus on problems within our business environment and fail to see opportunities right in front of us. When entrepreneurs focus on their problems – when people only think of what is wrong – they will only see problems and fail to see opportunities and solutions. It is advisable to make conscious efforts to turn things around. Spend your time and energy finding solutions rather than worrying about the problems. Worries do not solve problems. There is a saying that "when you think of problems, you will only attract more problems". Instead, when you think of solutions, your brain cells will initiate a positive spiral – attracting solutions and opportunities. Even if you do not find immediate solutions to your problems, you will certainly cultivate a positive and confident attitude to them.

> *"An optimist sees an opportunity in every calamity; a pessimist sees a calamity in every opportunity."*
>
> *– Winston Churchill*

Business owners must learn to develop an optimistic mindset and attitude to life – seeing more opportunities than problems within the operational environment. Winston Churchill is quoted as saying *a pessimist is one who sees calamities in all new situations while an optimist is one who sees opportunities in all calamities.* However, many Africans tend to focus, too often, on problems in their immediate environments. In doing so, they fail to see opportunities right in front of them. A piece of good advice that will be given is this: start your day by focusing on finding opportunities and solutions rather than problems.

Exploiting opportunities entails a willingness to take some risk. A piece of advice from a successful entrepreneur goes thus:

> Each day I try to do something I am a little not ready to do. I think that is how you grow. When there is that moment of 'Wow, I'm not really sure I can do this,' and you push through those moments, that is when you have a breakthrough.

It is often said that Africans, by nature, avoid risk as managers. If you are such a person, you will be satisfied with small gains and will be less likely to try new ways of doing things until other people have proved these new ways as good. Business owners who behave this way tend to adopt reactive rather than proactive strategies. They tend not to make major gains, but also avoid major losses.

Africans are also described as being short-term-oriented in their business decisions. This means they are more likely to place greater emphasis on short or quick gains, and emphasise leisure today rather working hard for major gains and pleasure in the distant future. Entrepreneurs that have this kind of orientation to business will not plough back much of their immediate earnings into their businesses and the chances of their businesses growing will be constrained.

As noted above, it is not wise for entrepreneurs to run after every business opportunity that they may identify. They need to decide on what areas of business activity they would want to concentrate. By focusing resources on specific business activities, they will be able to develop unique skills and capabilities that will allow them to compete more effectively and thereby grow their businesses.

Maintain Clear Intentions, Passion and Action

The management literature offers three guidelines for building growth-oriented entrepreneurial ventures (Kuada, 2016). These are popularly described as "**the three C's of growth**". They are:

1. **C**lear Intentions;
2. Passionate **C**ommitment; and
3. **C**onsistent Action.

The chances of making it big in business are remote if business owners do not have a clear intention. Words that are usually associated with intention include awareness, aspiration, proclivity, drive and commitment. The management gurus Hamel and Prahalad coined the concept "strategic intent" of business leaders in order to describe the importance of clear intentions. The concept "strategic intent" captures the essence of winning in business and sets a target that deserves personal effort and commitment, that is, it fosters a winner mindset not only in the owner of a business but also among key employees. This means that, without a strategic intent, business owners are likely to trim their ambitions to match their current resources and only spot opportunities that their immediate resources can capture. They will not stretch their imagination and find new solutions to existing problems if such solutions will require finding resources that they do not currently possess. Furthermore, they are not likely to identify opportunities that lie in the horizon or try to attain seemingly impossible goals.

Clear intentions must be backed by passion and commitment. Blending passion and commitment helps entrepreneurs to remain focused. It also provides them the reason to work hard. It is often said that passion is the fuel that ignites individuals' desires to work hard. When they are passionate about what they are doing, they will choose to make good use of every moment. They will see each day as an open opportunity for mastering skills and furthering their goals. Thus, when they have abundant passion, they will undoubtedly experience success. The more success they experience, the more they will increase their passion. In this way, passion rewards itself. It is through consistent and diligent work, coupled with patience and flexibility, that they can climb the ladder of success.

Intention, passion and commitment may not get entrepreneurs to their goals without action. Action is, therefore, seen as the platform on which success rests. Action empowers business owners and enables them to create their own future. Benjamin Disraeli is quoted as saying, "action may not always bring happiness; but there is no happiness without action". An action-oriented businessperson will always be proactive and will not wait for things to happen to him/her but rather make things happen. Stephen Covey (2004: 75) writes: "Our basic nature is to act, and not be acted upon. As well as enabling us to choose our response to particular circumstances, this empowers us to create our circumstances."

Furthermore, "Sustaining an audience is hard," Bruce Springsteen once said. "It demands a consistency of thought, of purpose, and of action over a long period of time." The cumulative results of our actions eventually create the circumstances that place us on the path of success. We admit that it is not possible to be action-oriented under all circumstances. When fate appears to be against a business owner, there may be the need to find means of energising oneself. A way to do this is to remind oneself consistently of one's goals in life.

Pay Attention to Growth-oriented Products and Services

A group of consultants in the United States of America – The Boston Consulting Group – once developed a model that classifies product classification in terms of "stars", "question marks", cash-cows" and "dogs". This model is reproduced in Figure 3.1 and provides a simple but useful overview of how companies can manage their product/service portfolios for sustained growth and profitability. We would like you to reflect on the guidelines in the model and learn from it.

"Stars" constitute a company's new/innovative products and services that provide values that its customers did not anticipate. They reflect the company's capacity to make decisions that explore opportunities that are barely incipient and, therefore, provide it with a first mover advantage. As long as the company can hold competitors off, it can establish itself effectively in that business area. It is, however, important to realise that such propositions are risky. The company is likely to be a pioneer in the specific line of business, and its potential customers many have no knowledge of how valuable the goods and services are. "Cash cows" are products and services that customers are familiar with and demand. This is an area where efficiency is highly important. Costs must be reduced, quality must be guaranteed, delivery systems and prices must be aligned to customer expectations, and customer complaints (if they occur) must be handled swiftly and satisfactorily. "Question mark" products and services are also known as *problem children*. They are classified as such because they have shown disappointing performances on the market. "Dogs" are goods and services that are no longer in high demand and require the company to spend more to serve its customers than the customers are willing to pay. It is always advisable to phase out such products quickly or re-launch them as new ones to new target customers who will see them as a "star" of a kind.

High Market Growth	Question Marks	Stars
Low	Dogs	Cash Cow
	Low	High

Market Share

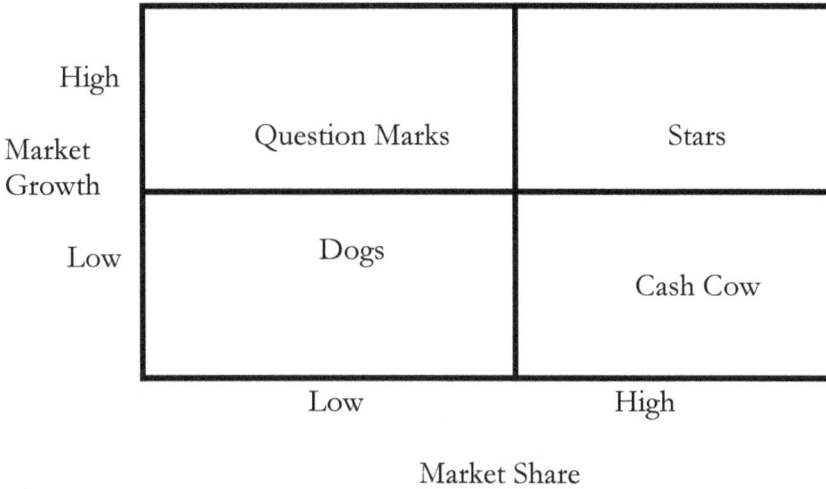

Figure 3.1: *The Boston Consulting Group matrix*

This matrix is a useful guide to how business owners can accelerate the growth of their businesses by balancing investments between exploration of new ideas and business lines and exploitation of established lines of business to make profit. As a business owner, one must always remember that growth requires cash input to finance added assets; the quicker one wants to grow your business, the more added cash one requires. Businesses can generate part of this cash from the existing line of business – their "cash cows". The more successful the existing lines of business are, the more money the businesses will have to invest in growth-related activities as long as the owners do not spend their profits frivolously. It is also important to remember that no line of business can grow indefinitely. Businesses must, therefore, plan and be on the lookout for high growth opportunities.

CHAPTER FOUR

Designing a Winning Strategy

Introduction

It has suggested earlier that, in order to grow their businesses, entrepreneurs need to have a clear view of the nature of business they want to undertake and a well-defined sense of where they want their businesses to be in the next five to ten years. To this end, they need a strategy that will enable them to deliver a unique value to their customers and position themselves uniquely in the chosen industry. However, when they read the management literature, they will note that strategy is a word with many meanings and there is no agreement among management scholars about how this may be done. Some scholars view strategy as a tool for implementing radical changes and creating a new vision of the future in which the company is a leader rather than a follower of trends set by others. Others see it as the determination of the basic long-term goals and objectives of an enterprise, and the adoption of courses of action and the allocation of resources for carrying out these goals. This chapter provides readers with some ideas about how to understand the strategic process and how to design and implement a winning strategy.

The Concept of Strategy

The following three questions will help entrepreneurs in formulating strategy: (1) goals – where do you want your business to go? (2) Strategic action – how is your business going to get there? (3) Evaluation – how will you know when you get there? The main emphasis of strategy is thus to enable an organisation to achieve a competitive advantage with its unique capabilities by focusing on present and future direction of the business.

Characteristics of Strategy

Some scholars see strategy as a planned set of activities, that is, the process is supposed to start with the formulation of what leaders of the organisation "plan" to do, and then it is followed by the actions. This conventional understanding implicitly assumes a separation between those with the talent and skills to formulate strategies and those who implement them. Planned strategies, therefore, have two essential characteristics: (1) they are made in advance of the actions to which they apply, and (2) they are developed consciously and purposefully. Top executives are expected to play a key role in the planning process because they have the skills and broader overview of their organisations' visions and directions. The implementation falls in the laps of middle and lower level managers who have the skills and knowledge of specific (tangible and intangible) resources in different parts of their organisations to take the required actions and make adjustments, where necessary.

A strategic planning process consists of a series of steps. The following are the most typical among them:

1. establishing a mission statement and key objectives for the organisation;
2. analysing the external environment (to identify possible opportunities and threats);
3. conducting an internal organisational analysis (to examine its strengths and weaknesses and the nature of current management systems, competencies and capabilities);
4. setting specific goals;
5. examining possible strategic choices / alternatives to achieve organisational objectives and goals;
6. adoption / implementation of chosen choices; and
7. regular evaluation of actions in terms of efficiency and effectiveness.

In contrast to a planning perspective on strategy, other scholars see strategy as a pattern in a stream of decisions. This means that, to them, strategies need not be deliberately planned, but can emerge as patterns or consistencies in streams of decisions and behaviours which managers and other key employees take. Following this line of thinking, the strategic process can be broken into the following four distinct phases: intended strategy, realised strategy, emergent strategy and deliberate strategy. **Intended strategies** are plans conceived by the top management team. **Realised strategies** constitute those parts of the intended strategies that employees are able to implement. Some parts of the intended strategies may not be implemented, possibly because assumptions made in the intended strategy have been found not to hold in reality. **Emergent strategies** represent all the strategic decisions that emerge from the complex processes in which individual managers adapt to changing external circumstances and make modifications in the intended strategies. Thus, the realised strategy is a consequence of deliberate and emerging factors that influence companies' behaviour.

The understanding is that the process of assessing and adjusting the direction of a business in response to changes in its operational environment need not be carefully planned in advance for it to be called a strategy. As long as managers are clear about their companies' objectives and are alert about changes that might affect the attainment of these goals and take steps that consciously respond to these changes or initiate actions that improve their chances of success, they will be considered to be managing their companies strategically. Strategic management, therefore, means making conscious choices that respond to current situations or anticipate the environment in which their businesses will be operating in the future. It requires what may be aptly described as *strategic awareness.*

From a business perspective, emergent strategies tend to encourage continuous improvements in costs, product quality, new product development, manufacturing processes and distribution to fulfil customers' expectations. Marketing managers adopting emergent approaches to strategy formulation are more likely to excite their key customers by taking advantage of situations as and when they occur to go beyond the immediate expectations of these customers without undue extra costs. However, it requires empowering salespersons to take initiatives in specific situations.

Most effective strategies tend to combine planning and control (**deliberate strategies**) with adaptation, flexibility and incremental learning. In other words, a company's actual strategy (its realised strategy) will most often be the outcome of the adaptation of a plan to emergent issues in the environment. This means the realised strategy can be very different from the strategy as planned.

Evaluation of Strategies

Whether one subscribes to the planning perspective or the strategic management perspective, it is important to bear in mind that a strategy can be neither formulated nor adjusted to changing circumstances without a process of strategy evaluation. Whether performed by an individual or as part of an organisational review procedure, strategy evaluation forms an essential step in the process of guiding an organisation.

The process of strategy evaluation consists of the following steps:

1. **Specifying Performance Benchmark** – Benchmarking is the process of comparing one's business processes and performance to the best performance within an industry. It helps management to identify industry leadership performance targets. Alternatively, the company can decide on its own internal performance benchmark against which the success or failure of the strategy can be evaluated.

   When fixing the benchmark performance target, it is essential to discover the special requirements for performing the main tasks outlined in the strategy and the capabilities (including resources) to perform these tasks. The performance indicator that best identifies and expresses the special requirements might then be determined to be used for evaluation. The organisation can use both quantitative and qualitative criteria for comprehensive assessment of performance. Quantitative criteria may include determination of net profit, return-on-investment, earning per share, cost of production, rate of employee turnover, etc. Among the qualitative factors are subjective evaluation of factors such as – skills and competencies, risk taking potential, flexibility, etc.

2. **Measurement of Performance** – The actual performance is then compared with the benchmark targets. In doing the performance measurement, the strategists must specify the acceptable degree of tolerance gap between the actual target and the accepted performance target.

3. **Analysing Variance** – If the analysis reveals gaps in the company's performance, it is important to analyse the variance, i.e. seek good

explanations for the differences. The explanations may be found in changes in either the internal or the external environments. The positive deviation indicates a better performance but it is quite unusual always to exceed the target. The negative deviation is an issue of concern because it indicates a shortfall in performance. It is possible that negative deviations are simply due to overoptimistic targets, in the first place.

4. **Taking Corrective Action** – Corrective actions must be planned and taken to close the gap between actual performance and the targets. In situations where the performance is consistently less than the desired performance, the management may be required to carry out a detailed analysis of the factors responsible for such performance. If it happens that strategic goals have been too high, it may make sense to lower the targets.

It is often argued that the critical factors that impact performance may not be directly observable or may take a long time to be noticed. By the time they become noticeable, it may well be too late for an effective response. Thus, it is important for managers to look beyond the obvious facts regarding the short-term performance of a business when they evaluate the effectiveness of their strategies. They must instead appraise those more fundamental factors and trends that govern success in the long run. In this way, they are more likely to capture the hidden influencing factors in good time.

The management literature teaches that any strategy (planned or emergent) must also satisfy four broad criteria:

1. **Consistency:** The strategy must not present mutually inconsistent goals and policies.
2. **Consonance:** The strategy must represent an adaptive response to the external environment and to the critical changes occurring within it.
3. **Advantage:** Strategy must provide for the creation and/or maintenance of a competitive advantage in the selected area of activity.
4. **Feasibility:** The strategy must neither overtax available resources nor create insoluble problems.

Staying on Track with a Strategy

The discussions above show that strategies will help entrepreneurs stay on track. This means their plans should be more than just a document that is kept in a drawer all year. They should use it as a way to check in each month to compare what they are doing within their businesses with how this is influencing their performance in both the short run and the long run. Entrepreneurs need to do some things on a routine basis in order to stay on track and avoid misusing their resources. Whenever business owners plan to take an action and commit resources, they must ask if the proposed actions make positive, neutral or negative contributions to the goals outlined in their strategy. In other words, will these actions get them closer to their goals or will they constitute distractions?

CHAPTER FIVE

Managing Efficiently and Effectively

Introduction

B usiness owners will be required to make several decisions that affect the profitability of their companies. Two main management concepts that they must bear in mind in these decisions are *efficiency* and *effectiveness*. Many managers find these two concepts rather confusing since they are frequently used interchangeably in everyday language. However, if managers understand their differences, this will help them in evaluating each decision in terms of how it will influence the profitability, growth and sustainability of their businesses. This chapter provides some clarity in the definition and usage of the concepts and explains their implications for management decisions.

Efficiency

The term "efficiency" is used in management to refer to the measurement of relationship between inputs and outputs, or how successfully inputs have been transformed into outputs in an organisation. In simple language, efficiency refers to doing things in a right manner – obtaining maximum output with minimum resources. Economists use the term "economic efficiency" to cover three sub-classifications of efficiency – productive efficiency, technical efficiency and dynamic efficiency. Productive efficiency is achieved when output is produced at minimum cost. This means that, if managers use resources in a productively efficient manner, it means they use the least necessary inputs to produce a given output of any commodity or service. In other words, they are productively efficient. The concept of productive efficiency includes both technical efficiency and dynamic efficiency. Technical efficiency refers to the extent to which it is technically feasible to reduce any input without decreasing the output, and without increasing any other input in the production process. Dynamic efficiency refers to the allocation of resources over time, including allocations designed to improve economic efficiency and to generate more resources. Dynamic efficiency may, therefore, directly influence the long-term survival of a business.

Effectiveness

The term "effectiveness" relates to the vision and mission that entrepreneurs have for their businesses, i.e. their dreams or what they desire to be the outcome of their business efforts. Effectiveness, therefore, measures the nature and level of accomplishment within a business. Entrepreneurs must see effectiveness in terms of what we call the **3Vs** – *Vision, Values* and *Voices*. Vision offers purposeful direction, i.e. having a destination. Without a vision, employees will end up duplicating their efforts, wasting their energy and, therefore, becoming inefficient in what they do. Values serve as the guideposts in every organisation, just as societal values inform citizens of a society about what they should see as "right" and "wrong". It means entrepreneurs' values will remind their employees of the inherent meaning of their jobs and provide them with guidelines on how they should go about their work. Voices give employees empowerment and allow them to relate closely with their managers, providing essential feedback on changes on the ground. Since realities on the ground change over time, it is important for managers to listen not only to the voices within themselves but also to those around them. Thus, effectiveness relates to entrepreneurs' capability to sense and know the "right things" to do and to guide all their employees to do those "right things" in the right manner. This also means the term "effectiveness" helps entrepreneurs keep the long-term sustainability of their businesses in mind and always be aware of the dynamics of the environment and adapt accordingly to them.

Any business or organisation may be assessed as having high or low degrees of efficiency and effectiveness. These assessments can be schematically presented in a 2 X 2 matrix as shown in Figure 5.1. The best run businesses are those in which decisions are made to ensure both high levels of effectiveness and efficiency. Such businesses demonstrate excellence in their operational performance as well as strategic management decisions. They will usually have costs under control, employees will be well aware of the tasks they have been delegated to perform, and these will be completed in a timely manner. This means most of the employees will show high levels of commitment and morale, and the long-term goals and vision of the organisation will be a source of inspiration and energy for their work.

		Effectiveness	
		High	Low
Efficiency	High	Consistently high performing organisations (demonstrate innovativeness and adaptability)	Organisations characterised by roles, authority structures and routines
	Low	Entrepreneurial and ideologically committed organisations	Consistently low performing organisations (lacking vision, direction, motivation and skills)

Figure 5.1: Efficiency and effectiveness dimensions of managerial decisions

If a business exhibits low levels of efficiency but is highly effective, it might survive, but its cost of operational management and inputs will be suboptimal and this will impact its overall performance. A business with such characteristics may be innovative and capture market shares from competitors, but might do so with high operational costs – barely breaking even or having very little profit. Usually, employee morale in such organisations will be high. But its overall survival will be doubtful. Businesses that are low in effectiveness but high in efficiency tend to focus on immediate tasks and their employees tend to exhibit high work discipline and skills that ensure optimal use of resources. Their short run operational (financial) performances will be high. But their employees will be mostly involved in routine tasks – their creative capacity will remain nearly unexplored.

Briefly, business owners must always aim at raising both their efficiency and effectiveness levels in their business. This means business owners must look at both immediate task performance and, at the same time, explore opportunities for long-term growth and sustainability. They must train their employees to focus their attention on efficiency-related decisions, making sure that the tasks are carried out with the minimum possible resources without overstraining their capacities or jeopardising their job satisfaction.

Implications for Business Strategies

Efficient entrepreneurs must be keenly aware of the limitations of their resources. The saying that "cut your coat according to the size of your cloth" applies here. They must develop strategies that serve specific segments of their markets and serve their customers well so that they become loyal to the businesses. This will cut their cost without sacrificing the quality of their services.

Another thing business owners may need to pay attention to is how efficiently their workers do their work. Waiting time is one measure of efficiency. They must make sure that their employees work in real time, that is, no one is kept waiting for information from other employees. When conducting meetings, it is important to have a policy that no meeting lasts for more than 45 minutes unless the issues being discussed have long-term implications for the business. This means there should be clear purposes and objectives for each meeting and determining if a meeting is the best way to address the issues.

Efforts must be made to use external services for things that other companies can do more efficiently than employees of the company. For example, instead of entrepreneurs employing their own accountants, they may consider having some of their accounting functions done by small accounting firms, if their fees are reasonable.

Remember to reward efficiency. If employees figure out how to perform a task in a smart way that will save money, it may be worthwhile giving them an extra vacation day or lunch on the company. This gesture is simple but raises motivation and increases commitment. Other employees will want to find other smarter ways of reducing costs.

Managing your business effectively means having a dream. Business owners must have a dream of being great in life. They must not be satisfied with making their first million dollars. To achieve this dream, the business owner must do what s/he is good at and build knowledge, skills and capabilities to achieve greater things. Never be defeated. They must remind themselves that losing a battle does not amount to losing the war.

CHAPTER SIX

Developing and Maintaining Trust with Business Partners

Introduction

S tudies of business relations in many African countries show that it is difficult for business people to enter into long-term relationships. They also find it difficult to enter into credit arrangements with one another when doing business. People simply do not trust one another. The lack of trust imposes additional costs on businesses, including shortages of critical inputs, delays in payments of wages and salaries to employees and non-delivery of goods to customers. African business owners, therefore, generally see the contract enforcement challenges as normal risks of doing business. Research has demonstrated that, when business owners understand and appreciate one another's viewpoints, they are able to arrive at working consensus and manage their relationships more effectively. The trust they build reduces the amount of resources that they spend on monitoring activities of one another. This, therefore, reduces the cost of operations and enhances business performance. It is, therefore, important for entrepreneurs to develop and maintain trust with their business partners as well as other individuals and institutions. This chapter offers some guidelines on how to initiate and develop trusting relationships.

Trust as a Foundation of Business

What is trust and how does one create it? David W. Johnson reminds us that trust is a word everyone uses, yet it is a complex concept difficult to define. In his view, making a choice to trust another person involves the perception that the choice can lead to gains or losses. Whether one gains or loses in a relationship depends upon the behaviour of the other person. By trusting another person, an entrepreneur implicitly believes that the person will act in a manner that will benefit the business. In other words, people who trust one another believe that their relationships are worth sustaining and, therefore, actively contribute to their continuity. Thus, trust leads to higher levels of loyalty and long-term collaboration between people. Fukuyama (1995), therefore, defines trust as the expectation of regular, honest and co-operative behaviour based on commonly shared norms and values.

Trust between business partners develops and grows through their exchange of experiences. When entrepreneurs engage in information exchange, joint problem-solving and mutual learning with their business partners over a period of time their trust in them will grow because both parties will show greater willingness to be flexible in their demands in the face of unanticipated changes. In that regard, trust complements written contracts between business owners with the understanding that a contract cannot be expected to address every eventuality and contingency faced in business.

Helpful Hints about Trust

1. Trust is a very complex concept to understand.
2. Trust exists in relationships, not in someone's personality; trust is something that occurs between people, not within people
3. Trust is constantly changing as two people interact.
4. Trust is hard to build but easy to destroy.
5. The key to building and maintaining trust is being trustworthy; the more accepting and supportive you are of others, the more likely it is that they will come to trust you.
6. Trust needs to be appropriate. Never trusting and always trusting are inappropriate.
7. Cooperation increases trust, competition decreases trust.

Source: Johnson, D. W. (1993). *Reaching out* (5th ed.). Boston: Allyn and Bacon. p. 67.

Note that trust is a risky undertaking in business. For trust to develop among business partners, they must be willing to let down their guards (as it is) and become vulnerable to see whether their partners will abuse that vulnerability. Put differently, trust lays the foundation for a mutual confidence among business partners that no party to an exchange will exploit the other's vulnerability. In the management literature, concepts such as honest dealing, openness, acceptance, support and dialogue have been used to describe antecedent conditions for trust building among collaborating business partners.

Trust-building is a learnable skill. Harvy Simkovits (President of Business Wisdom[3]) identifies 12 factors that can help build and sustain trust in a business relationship.

1. **Declaring Intent** – Intent is a fundamental motive people have for doing what they do. When people declare their intent to act in a particular way, they provide each other with words against which to measure their actions. The more each partner keeps his word, the more the overall confidence in them build in the relationship.
2. **Rapport** – If you can find things in common with another person, this will help you build rapport and help create fertile ground on which to build trust.
3. **Honesty** – This entails always telling the truth about how you see things; offering your true perspective on matters at an opportune time (when the other person is open to your thinking).
4. **Sincerity** – This entails demonstrating caring and unconditional positive regard to another person's point of view, even if you disagree with his/her perspective.
5. **Respect for Self and Others** – This entails always talking to and dealing with others as equals and never as if they were lesser than or greater than you; that is, never criticising them or belittling yourself; saying what you agree with before you say what you disagree with. You demonstrate respect in a relationship when you genuinely take your partner's feedback and viewpoints into account in making your decisions and when you do this on every occasion. Show sensitivity to their interests, wishes and needs. Value them and thank them.

---

[3] See http://www.business-wisdom.com/WhoWeAre.html

6. **Openness** – This requires fully hearing and understanding the other person's viewpoint; allowing yourself to be impacted by their needs and ideas. Do not punish mistakes. As they can happen, think and speak about them in a result-oriented and forward-looking way. Jointly look with others for solutions and implement actions to avoid that they will happen again.

7. **Competency** – This entails demonstrating your knowledge and know-how around matters of importance to the other person; also demonstrating your ability to get to what is most important to the other person and in being able to differentiate your point of view from theirs. Competence is demonstrated by doing the right thing, in the right way, for the right reasons, in the way that you said you would.

8. **Mutuality** – This requires always working to serve all parties' best interests; not being out just for yourself, or for just one or a few others. If your actions consistently create conditions where every party can win, this will work to bolster everyone's positive regard of you.

9. **Integrity** – This entails walking your talk (having alignment between your words and actions); taking your promises seriously and working sincerely to keep them.

10. **Reliability** – This means being consistent in your behaviour or in your way of being or acting.

11. **Admission** – If you make an error, gracefully admit it and explain in a simple way, how the error came about.

12. **Recovery** – When you need to break a promise, quickly inform the other person of the bad news, and apologise for not being able to fulfil the promise. You can then make a new promise in order to make it up to your partner.

As indicated above, it is always useful to remember that trust is a risky proposition and, therefore, not always appropriate. There are times when it is inadvisable to show high levels of openness and share resources or let down one's guard. However, if an entrepreneur has a *never trusting mindset*, this will make it nearly impossible for him to develop a business relationship that requires some degree of trust to become mutually beneficial.

CHAPTER SEVEN

Managing Employees Well

Introduction

Successful business owners are all aware that the most important resources they have are their employees. The way employees think and act and the manner in which they interact with other people (colleagues, customers, suppliers, competitors, government officials, etc.) and the relationships that they build through these interactions are all crucial for their own growth and their performance within the business. Their behaviours can improve their companies' chances of achieving their goals or, in some cases, constrain the prospects of achieving them. It is, therefore, important for business owners to think carefully about how they select and manage their employees. This chapter discusses issues relating to the selection of employees and the dismissal of those who hurt the business.

Decisions on Who to Employ

Employment of family members is a normal practice in small one-owner managed businesses in Africa. African business owners are, therefore, likely to experience some of the benefits and challenges of employing their relatives. As major breadwinners of the extended family, business owners are likely to be under immense and persistent pressure to hire family members even when there are no jobs for them. If they succumb to the pressure, their decisions will free them of the immediate stress that their elder siblings, uncles and aunts are likely to put on them. However, this will compromise the growth and viability of their businesses. Since family members employed come easily to the jobs and take their job security for granted, they scarcely feel obliged to improve their skills and do a good job. Non-family members that work for them are likely to adopt the same attitude as the family members in the business. After all, why should they work harder and go the extra mile if the family members do not do so. The net effect is that productivity will be low and opportunities will go unnoticed because no one, apart from the entrepreneurs themselves, will be seriously concerned with the survival of the businesses. In case the businesses collapse, the relatives may not suffer as much as the business owners. They will join businesses of other relatives that appear to be doing well or return to subsistence life on the family land.

The questions business owners should constantly ask themselves are these: Will my business grow if I employ a specific family member? How can I avoid the family pressure without losing face within the family?

> *"The best executive is the one who has sense enough to pick good men to do what he wants done, and self-restraint enough to keep from meddling with them while they do it."*
>
> — *Theodore Roosevelt*

Some successful business owners interviewed over the years have found creative solutions to the family pressure. They simply withdraw themselves from the extended family during the formative years of their businesses. This means that these business owners deliberately decide not to participate in most social and ceremonial functions of their families in order to avoid the predatory demands of the families during periods where cash flows in the businesses are limited and every single cent or penny is required to grow the business. They also cleverly avoid employing family members by assigning the personnel functions in their businesses to either a foreigner or someone outside their ethnic groups. These non-family managers have been able to adhere to the formal rules of employment (e.g. insistence on good qualifications and skills) and have disregarded family connections in the assessment of the qualifications of job applicants. When they have built substantial financial resources and are confident that family claims cannot jeopardise their organic growth ambitions, they re-join the family and participate fully in the social activities to which they are invited. The family then welcomes them with joy, just like the biblical prodigal son. However, not all business owners have the moral courage to adopt this approach.

Employing Talented Workers

It is important to find workers that have the required skills to address immediate problems in the businesses and keep the current business activities going. However, it is equally important to look ahead, i.e. into the future. Business owners must, therefore, employ talented workers – those who are creative enough to spot new opportunities and are willing to learn and grow with the business. Talented workers do not only find innovative solutions to business problems but are also active in creating new client relationships.

To start with, business owners must train themselves in identifying young and talented people and understand the context in which their talents can flourish. They must then provide these employees with the proper investment, guidance and opportunities for them to grow. There are several ways of going about this. One approach is to establish a good performance appraisal system, which not only evaluates a person's performance but also identifies his promotional potential.

Once business owners/managers have identified talented employees, they need to establish an effective method of developing and promoting them. Managing these people requires focus, resources and commitment. For example, employees must be encouraged to participate in setting the goals in their units or departments. This will give them greater motivation. However, progress in achieving these goals must be monitored. If the goals are achieved more quickly than expected, or if they have found more efficient solutions to problems they face in the process, they must be rewarded and encouraged.

Firing Employees that Hurt the Business

Firing employees can be a difficult decision for some managers and business owners. The main challenge for many managers is how to break the news firmly but gently, particularly when these employees have worked closely with the manager for years or if the employees are family members. This is understandable – it is an integral part of being a human being. We simply do not want to hear bad news or confront a bad situation squarely and find a solution.

Hanging onto the wrong people is not evidence of good business management. Managers may need to let some people go in order to help their business grow. However, they must give them a sufficient opportunity to redeem themselves before making the final decision. Managers, therefore, need to discuss concerns about the individual's poor performance with him or her. They also need to find out if the underlying causes of the poor performance are really from the worker or the work environment and if more training or guidance will help. Remember that employee incompetence may be the direct result of one's own management failure.

Here are some tips that managers may follow to make it a bit easier to make the difficult decisions of dismissal:

1. Provide each employee with written job descriptions that outline the minimum required for them to do. Discuss the job description with them and make sure that the contents are understood.
2. Do periodic evaluations of the employee's performance and discuss the assessment with them. Agree on what must be done for them to improve performance if you find their performance below expectation.
3. Inform them clearly that the consequences of continuous poor performance will be dismissal.
4. Avoid the following mistakes when dismissing an employee:

    a. **Do not talk about yourself:** If you say, "I know how you feel," or "I don't want to do this," you seem more worried about yourself than about the employee.
    b. **Do not sugar-coat:** Do not offer false praise and tell them all the reasons why you think they are great. It clouds the issue and can be confusing.
    c. **Stay calm and avoid being emotional:** Stick to the purpose of this meeting factually. Present the case to the employee as a necessary decision for the company and the employee.

CHAPTER EIGHT

Choosing an Appropriate Leadership Style

Introduction

S uccessful entrepreneurs know that they cannot achieve sustainable growth by bullying their employees. If they do so, they may be successful for a short while. However, their businesses may easily run into trouble because they have not provided their employees with a growth-oriented leadership. Thus, the choice of leadership style is important for superior performance. The importance of leadership for growth is also reflected in Johann Wolfgang Von Goethe's statement: "A great person attracts great people and knows how to hold them together." Thus, we can see leadership as the process of giving meaningful direction, meaning the direction provided by leaders must be seen by followers to be meaningful in terms of their own goals and ambitions in life.

This chapter provides insights into the types of leadership styles that will encourage employees to go the extra mile to help achieve the business goals. It is argued in the chapter that employees' perception of managers' and business owners' leadership style will determine how they behave at work in both the presence and absence of the managers. They base this perception on inferences and observations of past behaviours when they see their managers in action or what other employees say about the managers. This defines the psychological contract they have with their managers.

Task versus Employee-oriented Leadership Styles

Management scholars classify leadership styles into two broad categories: (1) task-oriented leadership style, and (2) employee-oriented style. A task-oriented leader is more concerned with getting the job done than seeking his subordinates' growth and personal satisfaction. They, therefore, supervise their subordinates very closely. Such leaders also believe that their employees will be motivated when they have clear-cut goals and know the rewards and punishments they will receive if they fulfil their tasks or fail to do so.

The employee-oriented leaders, on the other hand, tend to encourage friendly, trusting and mutually respectful relationship with their subordinates. They are also seen as being powerful and having a wide range of reach. Being powerful does not mean being despotic. It rather means using soft power to create a working environment that makes employees highly satisfied with their jobs. Studies have also shown a positive link between employees' job satisfaction and their desire to align their personal goals with those of the companies in which they work and a feeling of obligation to continue to work for the company.

The two styles of leadership can be practised by the same persons, depending on the leadership situations in which they find themselves or the maturity and competencies of the employees in which they are in charge. The term "maturity" is used here to mean the willingness and ability of a person to take responsibility for directing his or her own behaviour. In this sense, a mature subordinate is one who demonstrates a strong desire for achievement and willingness to accept responsibility. It means managers may adopt a task-oriented leadership style in handling newly appointed employees. However, as they become more mature, it is more appropriate for managers to become more supportive than instructive, giving them a free hand to handle tasks assigned them. Thus, managers must constantly assess the level of motivation, ability and task knowledge of employees to determine which leadership style combination they can successfully employ.

Lim and Lim (2013: 251), in their book *The Leader, The Teacher & You*, explain it this way: "If a leader sees his role as not just to lead well for today but to build well for the future, his best contribution then is as a teacher: identifying potential, recognising effort, encouraging ideas, and pursuing excellence with a continuous drive for the organisation to be the best it can be and the people to be the best they can be."

> _"The challenge of leadership is to be strong, but not rude; be kind, but not weak; be bold, but not bully; be thoughtful, but not lazy; be humble, but not timid; be proud, but not arrogant; have humor, but without folly."_
>
> — _Jim Rohn_

Empowerment: Giving Employees a Sense of Ownership

Business success depends much on what employees do when managers turn their back. Do they take their tasks seriously and exhibit a sense of responsibility to make things happen the way managers would want them to happen? Researchers have found out that the extent to which employees are committed to their work depends on the sense of ownership they feel. Ownership in this regard is a psychological factor and not a financial ownership. Employees are aware that they are not the owners of the business and the only financial reward they get is what the owners give them. However, if business owners forge a positive relationship with them and make them share the businesses' vision, they will make this vision part of their own value systems and put the achievement of these goals before their own self-interest. They will find meaning and satisfaction in working for the owners and will, therefore, protect the owners' interests even when they are away. This requires that owners exhibit enthusiasm and communicate clear and realistic expectations in their interactions with employees.

The dominant management practice in Africa is that employees are required to strictly follow instructions, rather than to think and find solutions to work-related problems that they face. They are expected to be thankful for the security, which their employers offer them in wages and benefits. Avoid this leadership style. Be bold enough to tell employees: "You are in control, solve problems you encounter in the best manner possible". Research has also shown that involving people early on during problem finding permits them to exercise their full creative potential. By transferring ownership of problems, managers will facilitate change in the mindsets of employees rather than impose it.

Mentoring Key Employees

Management literature encourages business owners and managers to have an active programme for personal growth and career development in their businesses. This requires providing ongoing training and, especially, the chance to be mentored. Studies have shown that employees that are mentored stay on the job longer than those that are left to sink or swim. If employees do not know what is expected of them or how they should go about their tasks, they feel frustrated and leave the company at the next available opportunity. Those who remain are those who do not have any real options. There is no doubt in our mind that business owners would want their employees to remain with their businesses, not simply because they do not have anywhere else to go. Management is not about a manager making decrees and followers responding to these decrees in a mechanical way. Frequent advice given to business owners and managers is that they should act as mentors and cheerleaders. That means they should adopt a hands-on approach in guiding new employees. As they gain and display more creative skills in their work processes, managers must change their style of leadership from a coaching role to being more facilitative. Cheerleading means that business owners and managers must act in a manner that makes employees feel good about themselves, they must spread joy.

The management literature identifies seven main roles a mentor can assume. But the appropriate role would depend on the needs of the specific employees of the company. Each of the seven roles is described below:

1. **Teacher:** As a teacher, a mentor needs to teach the mentee the skills and knowledge required to perform his/her position successfully. This role requires the mentor to have the required skills and knowledge. He must also have a rich pool of experience that would enable him to share the wisdom of past mistakes. Thus, the richer and more varied the mentor's experience, the better.
2. **Guide:** As a guide, the mentor helps the employees navigate through the inner workings of the organisation and make sense of the unwritten rules within the company. The inner workings of the organisation are simply the "behind the scenes" dynamics, or office

politics, that are not always apparent, but are crucial to know. The "unwritten rules" can include the special procedures an office follows, the guidelines that are not always documented and policies under consideration.

3. **Counsellor:** The role of counsellor requires the mentor to establish a lasting and open relationship. In order to create a trusting relationship, the mentor needs to stress confidentiality and show respect for the employees that confide in him, for example, by not disclosing personal information that employees share with him.

4. **Motivator:** Motivation is an inner drive that compels a person to succeed. Through encouragement, support and incentives, mentors can motivate employees to succeed. One of the most effective ways to encourage an employee is to provide frequent, positive feedback during assigned tasks. Positive feedback is a great "morale booster." It removes doubt and builds self-esteem that results in a sense of accomplishment.

5. **Sponsor:** A sponsor creates opportunities for employees. These opportunities can relate directly to the job or indirectly to the overall professional development of individual employees. The goal of the mentor is to provide as much exposure for the employee as possible, with a minimum of risk. Opportunities should challenge and instruct without destroying an employee's self-esteem.

6. **Coach:** Coaching is a complex and extensive process, and is not always an easy skill to perform. Specifically, coaching involves feedback. A mentor needs to give different kinds of feedback as the situation demands: positive feedback to reinforce behaviour and constructive feedback to change behaviour. Both types of feedback are critical to the professional growth of the mentee. Feedback should be frequent, specific and based on direct observation of the mentee (not second-hand information).

7. **Advisor:** This role requires the mentor to help the mentee develop professional interests and set realistic career goals. The mentor needs to think about where the mentee wants to go professionally and help set career goals. Career goals should be specific, time-framed, results-oriented, relevant, reachable and flexible to accommodate the changing dynamics of the organisation.

> *"A leader takes people where they want to go. A great leader takes people where they don't necessarily want to go, but ought to be."*
>
> —*Rosalynn Carter*

The ACHIEVE Model

Hersey[4] identified seven variables regarding effective performance management: ability, understanding, organisational support, motivation, performance feedback, validity and environment. They describe these variables in their "ACHIEVE" – model. It consists of the following:

1. **A**bility: This refers to the employee's knowledge, experience and skills, which are the abilities to complete the specific task successfully. As noted earlier, strengthening employees' ability entails providing them with task-relevant education and facilitating their acquisition of task-relevant experience and task-relevant skill.

2. **C**larity: This refers to an understanding and acceptance of what to do, when to do it, and how to do it. Employees must know clearly what the major goals and objectives are, how they should be accomplished and their priority. Employees should be encouraged to raise questions for further clarification on things they are not sure about.

3. **H**elp: You must always make sure that your employees have all the help they need to accomplish an assigned task. This may include issues such as adequate budget, suitable equipment and facilities.

4. **I**ncentive: You must always remember that not all people could be equally motivated to accomplish all tasks. External incentives are always useful.

---

[4] See Hersey, Paul (2007). *Management of Organisational behaviour*, Ninth edition, Upper Saddle River, p.72

5. Evaluation: An evaluation system includes day-to-day performance feedback and informal and formal periodic reviews. A good evaluation system can make employees clear about their performance and to improve the performance further.

6. Validity: Your decisions must always be tested against the existing laws and moral codex of the country. This will provide you with legitimacy within your industry and make your employees proud to be working in your company.

7. Environment: Always keep changes with the external operational environment in mind when you make strategic decisions.

Box 8-1

The Personality of a Good Leader

1. Learn to be strong, but not rude. Some people mistake rudeness for strength. Do not be that type of leader.

2. Learn to be kind, but not weak. Kindness must not be mistaken for weakness. Kindness is a certain type of strength. For example, you must be kind enough to tell your employees the truth about their performance and what they can do to improve it.

3. Learn to be bold, but not a bully. To build your influence, you've got to be willing to take the first arrow, tackle the first problem, and discover the first sign of trouble.

4. Learn to be humble, but not timid. Do not mistake timidity for humility.

5. Learn to be proud, but not arrogant. The worst kind of arrogance is arrogance from ignorance. It's when you don't know that you don't know.

6. Learn to accept the fact that not everyone will like you. According to Colin Powell (former US secretary of State), "trying to get everyone to like you is a sign of mediocrity".

Some scholars argue that a good leader's true identity is revealed when he leads from within. This means that the leader is able to implant his values in the inner core of his followers' lives and is able to generate capability, capacity, confidence and the zeal to accomplish feats beyond the remotest fantasies of the leader. This means followers live their own and bring their own dreams to bear on their actions, using the fundamental values of their mentor as a platform. In this way, the leader achieves continuity and change in the lives of his followers. This advice is also appropriate for business owners.

CHAPTER NINE

Communicating with Maturity

Introduction

Communication is the most important key to a business manager's success. Open and effective communication facilitates the day-to-day operations within a business, ensuring that everything runs smoothly and reducing waste of time on unessential issues. Managers must learn how to be effective, compelling communicators. However, African managers are very often accused by their employees of not communicating clearly enough regarding roles, goals, expectations and the importance of specific behaviours for achieving their goals. Some actually "over-communicate", that is, they communicate inappropriately through outbursts, anger or blaming. They also often fail to communicate the vision in a meaningful way.

Business owners and their managers must learn how to communicate with thoughtfulness and the knowledge that inspire employees to exert themselves in their work and exceed expectations. This entails developing an ability to manage emotions and to assess the emotional state of others in order to exert positive influences on their behaviour. This style of communication will result in fewer disagreements and less drama in relationships with your employees as well as government officials and business associates.

This chapter offers some general observations of the requirements of good communication and some tips about how managers can improve their ability to communicate.

The Nature of Communication

The word "communication comes from the Latin word "communis", meaning "to share or to participate". Thus, communication involves the effort of people to get in touch with one another and to make them understood. In business, it is often said that about 75% of the manager's time is spent on communicating business decisions to others, including strategies, targets, rules and policies. However, effective communication is not a one-way transmission; it is a dialogue. That is when information is shared accurately between two or more people, with receivers responding with a view to seeking clarity or sharing other types of information that enrich the pool of knowledge available to the participants in the communication process. Successful communication also tends to strengthen the feeling of togetherness between the participants in the communication. Communication is, therefore, a social activity.

It will be a good idea to learn to adapt the managers' communication style to the persons they are interacting with or to the situations in which they find themselves. Their goal must be to encourage the people they communicate with to react to meet the goals of the communication. When they communicate, they must be aware that the target audience may be either within the company or outside. The location of the target audience may influence the purpose of the communication. Internal communication may have one or a combination of the following objectives:

1. Bind employees together and improve morale in the business.
2. Facilitate planning and co-ordination of business activities.
3. Help employees make the right decisions.

External communication may be directed at employees in other businesses and organisations that the company relates to as well as customers. Managers may want to persuade them to behave in a way that helps them achieve their business goals. It pays in every communication to see the person as if he or she is a king or a queen. It is important to treat the person with respect and dignity. Those who do so will nearly always get a positive response from the individual. This is a golden rule in communication. This is what some people refer to as communicating with maturity. The understanding is that, because maturity affects emotional control and reasoning, it affects individual's ability to work together and to make successful joint decisions.

Managers must remind themselves that their employees tend to emulate how they (employees) see them (managers) act and communicate. If employees see that their managers use an active listening style and an empathetic tone with customers, they are more likely to do the same. When managers are perceived as being open to the ideas of others and often praise others, the employees tend to follow suit.

Practise Active Listening

An important aspect of communication is the ability to listen. Active listening should always be your goal. It is important to focus on both the verbal and nonverbal language of people with whom managers interact. Active listening involves concentrating only on the speaker and ignoring outside interruptions. Active listeners also refrain from interrupting, give the speaker time to finish, and show they are listening by nodding or smiling.

Listening is particularly crucial when emotions are high. This could be in situations when employees or customers interact with a manager in a state of anger, resentment or excitement. Generally, people feel acknowledged when others validate their feelings. If people ignore the feelings of those with whom they relate, this can create a distance between them and may negatively affect the working environment in the company.

Listening is also particularly important when employees are sharing ideas. When managers stop listening to ideas, employees stop offering them. That means managers are essentially cut off from the creativity and expertise of their employees.

It is, therefore, advisable to spend a little bit of time each day learning, reading and practising essential communication techniques. It may seem difficult to become an excellent communicator; however, with practice, one will soon observe improvements in one's communication skills.

Ego and Communication Style

The style of communication will also affect the degree of motivation and commitment of employees to their duties. The managers' preferred style of communication may be an attribute of individuals' personality. Berne's (1964) Transaction Analysis (TA) theory provides a useful frame of reference for understanding the role of personality in interpersonal communication processes. He argues that individuals' personality can be seen in their manifestation of three ego states: (1) child ego state, (2) parent ego state, and (3) adult ego state. These ego states represent consistent patterns of feeling, thinking and experience and do not relate to age or family status.

The "child ego state" is a metaphor that describes behaviours originating from impulses, that is, unpredictable emotional outbursts that are normally associated with children. Individuals whose dominant behaviours are conditioned by their child ego state are likely to change abruptly from manifesting hatred for a host culture to love, depending on the situation and their temperament at a given time. Their non-verbal expression may include scowl, frown, grumbling, shouting and giggling.

If managers' behaviours derive mainly from the "parent ego state", they are most likely to be judgmental and critical in their interpersonal communication settings. They are also likely to use such words as "should" and "ought to" in their oral communication when referring to the behaviour of other people. They may also be likely to be frequently seen shaking their heads, patting people on their shoulders or pointing a finger accusingly. In other words, they tend to put themselves in the parent position when dealing with other people. Such an orientation is unlikely to create a good atmosphere for interpersonal communication, particularly if the people they are communicating with are sensitive about their statuses and positions and expect to be treated with utmost respect.

The "adult ego state" is characterised by encouraging people to be less hasty in their conclusions and willing to seek information and knowledge about various issues with which they are involved before making decisions. If managers communicate from an "adult ego state", they are likely to be more patient and restrictive in their choice of words and emotional expressions. They frequently use the following expressions: "Is that right", "Is it okay to do?", "What would you say to this suggestion?", etc.

As individuals, we are likely to demonstrate any of these ego states, and often shift unknowingly from one to the other. For instance, in front of our boss, we may exhibit a child ego state, whereas we will exhibit a parent ego state or adult ego state towards our subordinates. All the three ego states add value to our lives; however, when one of them disturbs the equilibrium, an analysis and reconfiguration are desired. We all find ourselves in situations where we may think that we can elicit a response from someone, or if we can get them to do what we want, then this can give us a great power buzz and make us feel that we are in control. This may make the people we interact with a bit insecure and the insecurity might trigger resentment. However, they instead respond to others by appreciating and listening to them, using respectful tones, perceiving the facts, considering alternatives, having a long-term view of the suggestions made, and behaving as an adult; these emanate from their adult ego state.

The Story of the Blind Beggar

This story is told by Lim and Lim (2013) in their book *The Leader, The Teacher & You*. It illustrates the power of communication in changing human behaviour. Reflect on it.

A blind boy sat on the steps of a building with a hat by his feet. He held up a sign that said, "I am blind, please help me."

There were only a few coins in the hat. A man walking by took a few coins from his pocket and dropped them into the hat. He then took the sign, turned it around, and wrote several words. He put the sign back so that everyone who walked by could see it.

Soon, the hat began to fill up. A lot more people were giving money to the blind boy.

That afternoon, the man who had changed the sign came to see how things were. The boy recognised his footsteps and asked, "Were you the one who changed my sign this morning? What did you write?"

The man said, "I only wrote the truth. I said what you said but in a different way."

What he had written was: "Today is a beautiful day and I cannot see it."
What made the difference?
The first sign simply asked for help. But the second sign reminded all those who passed by and could see how privileged they were to see and enjoy the beautiful day.
An important lesson to learn from this story is this: "Think differently. There is always a better way to communicate. The manner you communicate to others determines the response you get from them".

CHAPTER TEN

Engaging in Fast Learning

Introduction

It is generally acknowledged in management literature that knowledge is an important source of competitive advantage. This requires learning. Learning is a process of acquiring and sharing information, as well as reflecting on the information acquired. This process must be grounded in the actions of everyday situations. Knowledge acquired in a given situation can be and are transferred to similar situations. Knowledge management scholars inform that social processes influence the way we think, perceive, solve problems, and share knowledge with others. We frequently learn by making mistakes. In business, just as in other fields of life, learning from others is one of the key mechanisms to generate new knowledge. This chapter offers some guidelines on how to learn.

Learning and Absorptive Capacity

Absorptive capacity is the term management scholars use to describe the ability people have to understand the knowledge received from others.

It is often said that when people *do* want to learn something new, they tend to assess their ability to absorb the new knowledge and match this against the outcomes of applying the new knowledge. However, very often, our assessment of ourselves (what we know and don't know, skills we have and don't have) can be inaccurate. We frequently think that we know a lot more about running our business than we actually do. We are, therefore, not prepared to invest time and resources to upgrade our knowledge in any specific way. This self-deception surely diminishes any appetite for development. This blocks our minds and reduces our absorptive capacity.

Another factor that reduces our desire to learn is the tendency we all have to keep within our comfort zones. Once we become good or even excellent at some things, we rarely want to go back to being *not* good at other things. However, the first step to learning something new is to accept the inadequacy of one's existing pool of knowledge. To learn fast, business owners must accept that their knowledge in some aspects of running their businesses can be improved. They must not feel embarrassed by this; rather, they should accept it as the best opportunity they have to grow their businesses.

Four Stages of Learning/Hierarchy of Competence

The learning literature identifies four stages of learning – or what some scholars call the hierarchy of competence. This learning model suggests that individuals are initially unaware of how little they know, or unconscious of their incompetence. As they recognise their incompetence, they consciously acquire a skill and then consciously use it. Eventually, the skill can be utilised without it being consciously thought through: the individual is then said to have acquired unconscious competences._These are explained briefly below.

1. Unconscious Incompetence

This is a situation when business owners or their managers are doing something wrong and do not know that the approach they are adopting is wrong. This means they do not know that they do not have the skills and competencies required to accomplish the task. At its best, this can be described as 'blissful ignorance' and, in rare cases, is a great enabler of innovation, as it allows people to attain results that conventional approaches may prevent them from achieving. However, generally this is not the case and 'not knowing what you do not know' is a real disabler of advancement.

2. Conscious Incompetence

Although the individual does not understand or know how to do something, he or she does recognise the deficit, as well as the value of a new skill in addressing the deficit. The making of mistakes can be integral to the learning process at this stage.

3. Conscious Competence

The individual understands or knows how to do something. However, demonstrating the skill or knowledge requires concentration. It may be broken down into steps, and there is heavy conscious involvement in executing the new skill.

4. Conconscious Competence

The individual has had so much practice with a skill that it has become "second nature" and can be performed easily. As a result, the skill can be performed while executing another task. The individual may be able to teach it to others, depending upon how and when it was learned.

This model helps managers understand the emotions that they will experience during the learning process and helps them manage their expectations of success, so that they do not try to achieve too much, too soon. It will also help them stay motivated when times get tough when learning new skills. It is also useful in coaching and training situations, because it allows them to be in touch with what their employees are thinking and feeling. They can then help them understand their emotions as they learn new skills and encourage them when they are feeling disillusioned.

Learning in the Community of Employees

Management scholars also say that companies learn through their employees and most of the learning takes place in specific work situations where employees interact. However, to learn, we first need to *unlearn* some of the knowledge we already have. Unlearning is a process through which we discard obsolete and misleading knowledge, replacing them with new knowledge.

When people see that they can do better than they are actually doing, they are usually motivated to find out what they are doing wrongly and what they can do to correct their errors. Correcting errors provides a learning experience that ensures that similar problems can be effectively addressed in the future. However, just correcting errors will not enable people to do things extraordinarily or improve their performance in comparison to their immediate competitors. They must instead continuously ask the following question: "What has prevented me and my company from questioning practices that have resulted in the errors in the first place?" This will help them take a serious (somewhat painful) look at their habits in the company to help them change their mindsets and help their employees change theirs as well. With a new mindsets they will do things differently and improve their fortune.

CHAPTER ELEVEN

Generating and Sustaining Positive Human Energy

Introduction

Emotional knowledge is a new management concept. Business leaders are encouraged to find ways to energise themselves and their workers, to recoil to rooms of silence and to engage in meditation and self-reflection in order to sharpen their intuitive capabilities to make decisions that could change the fortune of their companies. Those who accept and apply the concept of emotional knowledge maintain that human energy is most effectively used when it supplements, not supplants, rational decision-making techniques. These scholars draw distinction between negative and positive energies that derive from some specific human attributes. The negative attributes include greed, selfishness, manipulation, secrecy, distrust, anxiety, self-absorption, fear, burnout and feelings of abuse that tend to derail organisational efforts. Positive attributes include appreciation, collaboration, virtuousness, vitality and meaningfulness. Employees in such businesses are characterised by trustworthiness, resilience, wisdom and humility. This chapter offers some insights into this line of thinking.

Characteristics of Human Energy at the Workplace

It is often argued that, when employees are managed as "resources", they tend to do what other resources do: they become depleted or absent – they burn out or move to another company. If this happens to a company, it will result in substantial investment losses (including knowledge leakages). Thus, the concept of "human assets" has been introduced into the literature to emphasise the inherent positive characteristics of employees. Managed as "assets", employees are expected to flourish and grow in value. The concept of human energy or fundamental life condition is another concept that has recently entered into the management literature. This concept takes us beyond *who* we are as humans as reflected in our rational being and belief systems and gets us closer to an understanding of that aspect of our being that makes us uniquely and typically human. Religious scholars describe this aspect of human life as the human spirit or soul.

In physics, energy is the ability or capacity to do work or to produce change. It is common for energy to be converted from one form to another. However, the law of conservation of energy (a fundamental law of physics) states that, although energy can be changed in form, it can neither be created nor destroyed. Therefore, understanding psychic energy is a matter of assessing not only the conditions of the energy but also the circumstances that determine, inhibit and generate certain conditions of energy. It also requires an understanding of the consequences of particular energy conditions and the kind of transformation processes that energy can potentially undergo in order to produce change.

Energy generally exists in a *latent* form and is - as such - not visible to people, that is, human beings are not aware of their energy until some external causes trigger it into a *manifest* form. Latent energy turns into manifest energy within organisations through interaction. As people interact, they experience the flow of energy within and between each other. The flow may be experienced as more or less intensive and over short or long periods of time. But the interaction also produces transformation within and between people who interact. In other words, there is a simultaneous process of transformation and manifestation of energy occurring through interaction processes among employees. It is this simultaneity of transformation and manifestation that produces differences in the dynamic capabilities of businesses.

We encourage readers to think for a moment about how they felt during the latest business meeting they attended and think about how the people at the meeting behaved. This will help them get a picture of how human energy manifests itself in practice. In situations where the energy in which the meeting is embedded is marked by strength and intensity, all the participants tend to be well prepared and focused. Everybody contributes to the discussions with openness and joy. Important decisions are made swiftly based on a thorough and swift dialogue.

However, if the strength of the energy is low, most of the participants will appear to be less prepared and key persons may be absent from the meeting. Many participants may feel disorganised and frustrated, doing all other things than focusing on the central points of discussion, for example, glancing through other papers, checking mails, leaving to get some more coffee, etc.

Energy Transmitters and Human Life Tendencies

As noted earlier, individuals are transmitters of energy within organisations. The transmission takes place during interpersonal relations and/or group interactions. Language and emotions combine to transmit the latent energy inherent within the individuals to one another. A typical situation in which energy transmission occurs within organisations is during interactions between staff at different levels of organisational hierarchy. The transmission process is often self-reinforcing. This means positive energy manifestation sets off a spiral of positive energies, while an initial negative energy manifestation produces the reverse effect.

Whether or not an individual's behaviour manifests an invigorating (positive) or weakening (negative) energy in an organisation or a group will depend on four sets of factors: (1) the *basic life tendencies* of the individual; (2) the events in his/her *life history;* (3) the *manifested collective energy* within the ambient environment (e.g. organisation); and (4) the *socialisation process* or culture that has shaped his/her life. The diversity of individual life tendencies provides each organisation with unique potentials for transmission of energy. It is this feature that defines the degree of organisational agility, as well as the non-immutability and non-substitutability of organisational resources. This means the ability of one organisation to exhibit superior competitive capabilities over other organisations within a given industry and to manage linkages (local and international) may be understood through the psychic energy construct.

Individual life tendencies are shaped by events from history. Each individual's journey through life is laced with challenges from birth to death. During this span of life, the cumulative experiences (ways in which individuals tackle the complex set of events in their lives) provide the foundations of their basic life tendencies. Asian religious scholars suggest that some of these events may predate birth itself. They are also shaped by socialisation and upbringing, i.e. the culture of the societies within which a particular individual has been raised. This is combined (at work) with the patterns of socialisation and the rules of accepted behaviour that have guided the individual's life experience. Psychologists attempt to understand these basic tendencies as the individual's personality.

Borrowing from Asian religious philosophies, the fundamental life tendencies of human beings can be analytically classified into 10 hierarchically ordered categories: hell, hunger, animality, anger, tranquillity, rapture, learning, realisation, altruism and wisdom/compassion. The quality and value of the energy manifested through each life condition are different. Each life condition is thus considered to have its own type of catalytic potential. Technically speaking, the states of life condition are the fields through which the energies flow, not the psychic energies themselves. They are like doors which may be unlocked by certain conditions and circumstances. The 10 life conditions can be divided in two broad groups – the lower level life conditions and the higher level life conditions, as explained below.

The Lower Level Life Conditions

The first six states are called the *six lower level life conditions*. These are hell, hunger, animality, anger, tranquillity and rapture. They have in common the fact that their emergence or disappearance is governed by external circumstances. Take the example of a firm with a strong desire to find someone to invest in a new risky idea. That desire reflects an organisational life condition akin to "hunger". If a manager finds an investor, especially after a long search, a feeling of ecstasy and fulfilment ensues, i.e. they find themselves in a state of rapture. By and by, potential rivals with similar ideas appear on the scene, and the managers become jealous (i.e. in a state of anger). The manifestation of the anger may drive the venture partner away. Crushed by despair (i.e. in a state of hell), the managers are filled with frustration. In this way, many of us – individually as well as collectively (in organisations) – spend time shuttling back and forth among the six lower level life conditions without ever realising that we are being controlled by our reactions to the environment.

The Higher Level Life Conditions

The next two states – *learning* and *realisation* – come about when top management of an organisation recognise that everything experienced in the six lower life conditions of the organisational life is impermanent, and they begin to seek some enduring or higher level vision that can drive its organisational life and development. These two states plus the next two – *altruism* and *compassion/wisdom* – may be called higher life tendencies. Unlike the six lower tendencies, which are passive reactions to the environment, these four higher tendencies are achieved through a deliberate effort – a proactive strategic orientation based on ethical probity. Organisations whose manifest collective energies are guided by the four higher life conditions are no longer prisoners to their own reactions.

Building Positive Human Energy

One of the greatest challenges business owners and their managers face and have to process is the distraction of the mind. While their efforts are focused on getting one job done, their mind may keep on reminding them of the many other things that they need to do. Employees face similar problems. This reduces the overall positive energy that they all devote to accomplishing important tasks and becoming productive in their businesses. A solution to this distraction is to nurture the energy base of the business through positive interactions. Some people call this "relational energy" management.

Interactions are energising in several ways. When business owners show genuine love for their jobs and are present and attentive when they interact with employees and demonstrate a general happy attitude to their work, they will energise many employees. They will give them hope even in situations when things may not seem to be moving in the right direction. In this regard, they will become important sources of relational energy at the workplace. The more people they energise, the higher their work performance. This occurs because people want to be around them. They attract talent, and people are more likely to devote their discretionary time to their projects. This is why some businesses succeed while others fail within the same environment.

CHAPTER TWELVE

Managing Time Effectively

Introduction

Since we all have only 24 hours a day, the manner in which we use every minute of the day is important to our success as individuals and as business owners and managers. We know from experience that it is just as ineffective to waste time on things that are not urgent, as it is to waste it on unimportant things. This chapter offers some illustrative examples that can help organise managers' time effectively and help employees do the same. Managers that take the guidelines here seriously and put them into effect will develop a new business culture that will raise employee productivity and performance without any extra effort or resources.

The Key to Effective Time Management

The word "urgent" is a decisive term in time management. Any task business owners and managers label "urgent" will attract immediate attention, no matter how trivial it may be. It acts as a tyrant – urging people unceasingly to pay attention to it. If they do not, they will go through the rest of the day or week with a sense of guilt. It is, therefore, important for managers to decide which activities merit the label "urgent". This is the first step in taking control over how they spend their time.

Another important word in time management is "important". If managers label a task important, they are compelled to devote a substantial proportion of their time to it. They can only find enough time to the important tasks if they remove "urgent" labels that they have attached to unimportant tasks. The time saved then makes it possible for them to attach urgent labels to important tasks that are being neglected.

The wisdom managers can derive from this simple principle illustrated in Figure 12.1.

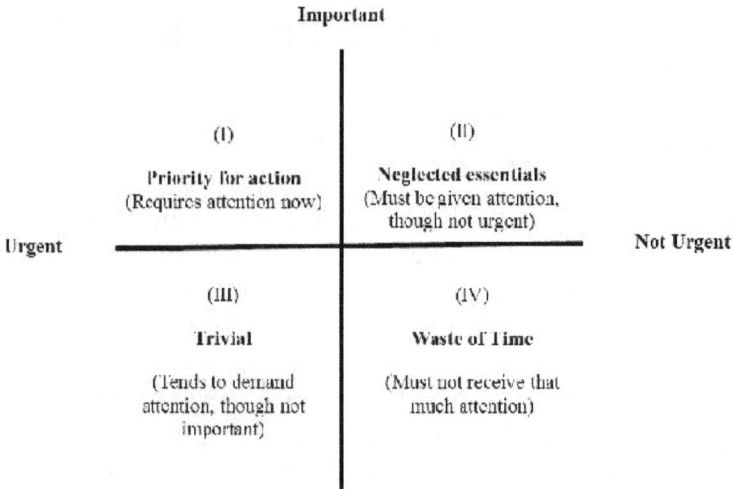

Important

(I)	(II)
Priority for action	**Neglected essentials**
(Requires attention now)	(Must be given attention, though not urgent)

Urgent · Not Urgent

(III)	(IV)
Trivial	**Waste of Time**
(Tends to demand attention, though not important)	(Must not receive that much attention)

It is obvious that managers must devote time to tasks that they place in quadrant **I** – doing things that are both important and urgent. Conversely, they spend as little time as possible on things that are neither important nor urgent (i.e. quadrant **IV**).

There is a tension between the other two quadrants. Urgent things demand attention – even when they are not important (quadrant **III**). On the other hand, important things – even when they appear not to be urgent (quadrant **II**) – ought to get done. Since the urgent label is always compelling, managers are likely to put important tasks on hold, while time is absorbed with the unimportant.

One needs to think about how much time one spends entertaining visitors (friends and family members) that walk into one's office without any prior invitation. Social norms label such visits "urgent", although not important in the light of our business obligations. How does one deal with such visits? Is one bold enough to tell the visitors that one will not have time for them? This is a major challenge that African managers face. The way managers deal with their visitors will guide their employees as to how they should treat similar visitors and help correct the ineffective use of time in the business.

Managers are advised to label things they want done "urgent" and remove the label "urgent" from all the things on which they do not want to waste time. In this way, they will not have any guilty feeling in paying attention to the urgent tasks, since everything that is labelled urgent is now also important. Thus, paying attention to the urgent means that all one's time is spent in the priority area on things that are both urgent and important. Getting focused means raising the urgency on important things that have been pushed to the bottom of the pile. To get neglected essentials into the priority area, they must be labelled urgent. This labelling exercise is a simple trick that produces wonderful results.

Delegation and Time Management

Learning how to delegate will help business owners save time, and at the same time motivate and train employees. In this way, they will be able to achieve more without burning themselves out. It is also a first step in training their assistants and free up time to take on new responsibilities in order to grow their businesses.

There are three main concepts that should guide the delegation process: _authority_, _responsibility_ and _accountability_. They need to remember that, when they delegate, they share authority with the employee to whom they have delegated a particular task. Authority is the power they give to the employee to act and make decisions within designated boundaries. Responsibility refers to the act of carrying out the task. When delegating a task, managers share the responsibility of completing the work with the employee to whom they have delegated the task. Their responsibility is to provide clear-cut instructions on what work needs to be done, while the employee is responsible for figuring out how the task should be completed. During the delegation of a task, the accountability of the task transfers from the manager to the employee. Accountability here is the act of being liable for one's actions and decisions.

The first step in the delegation process is to carefully select which task to delegate. Not every task is an ideal candidate to delegate. Some of the tasks that are placed in quadrant III may be considered for delegation. The second step is to choose the right persons to perform the tasks. This step can be one of the hardest steps. It takes time and effort to find a person who possesses all the traits and skills required for the job. The person not only needs to have the right technical skills or expert knowledge, but also needs to be trustworthy and have the time to take on the additional work. In addition, the person needs to have similar values and ethics to the person delegating the task. The next step in the delegation process is to monitor the progress of the knowledge and skill transfer. Initially, the manager doing the delegation will spend some time in monitoring the work process and make themselves available for questions and provide feedback on the progress of the work to guarantee the delegation process is successfully completed.

CHAPTER THIRTEEN

Putting Customers at the Centre of Management Decisions

Introduction

Customer-centrism became a popular buzzword in business magazines in the 1980s and 1990s and is still extensively used to date. A customer-centric approach to business management simply means that the customer is at the centre of all decisions that managers and employees take and the manner in which they behave towards customers. This business philosophy is also described as *market orientation* in academic literature. Market-oriented companies tend to develop business cultures that depend on organisation-wide learning systems. It means all employees continuously learn and reflect on their daily interactions with their customers and share these experiences with other employees through well-organised systems of information generation and sharing. In some companies, the degrees of customer orientation shown by employees in their interactions with customers are measured, and employees who show higher degrees of customer orientation are rewarded accordingly. This means that businesses that are very customer-oriented will have a sustainable advantage over their immediate competitors.

This chapter shows how customer orientation can help entrepreneurs develop a strong business management culture that can enhance the performance of their businesses. The chapter begins with an outline of typical customer expectations and the dominant characteristics of a market-oriented company in general. We also introduce readers to another set of popular concepts in business strategy – Red Ocean and Blue Ocean strategies. Thus, the chapter offers a new set of business vocabularies that can help readers to think through their business strategies.

Customer Expectations

Expectation can be defined as product characteristics and the level of service the customer hopes to receive. It is a "wished for" level, that is, a combination of what customers believe can and should be delivered in the context of their personal needs. The marketing literature refers to this as a desirable expectation, i.e. reflections of the hopes and wishes of customers. The desirable expectation may also be termed *ideal expectation*, i.e. an expectation of what "perfect" service should be.

However, most customers are realistic and appreciate the fact that companies may not be able to deliver the desired level of service each time. Hence, they have a tolerance level or "threshold" level of expectations. In the marketing literature, this is referred to as the "zone of tolerance" or "adequate service level", i.e. the range of service performance that customers consider satisfactory. In other words, they may accept some performance variation within that mentally defined range.

When customers select a product or a company to deliver the services they need, they normally have a prediction of what level of service they are likely to receive based on either of two sets of information/knowledge or a combination of both:

1. Prior experience of customers with a specific service provider, with competing service providers in the same industry, or with related services in different industries.

2. If they have no relevant prior experiences, customers may base their pre-purchase expectations on word-of-mouth comments, news stories or the service provider's own marketing efforts (mass and non-mass media communication).

Marketing scholars argue that most customers have the following five key expectations from products and services they consider buying:

1. **Nature of products and services:** Customers expect the products and services they are offered to be appropriate to their needs. The size and frequency of purchase may influence the type of products or services customers consider to be appropriate. A customer that

makes a small, spontaneous purchase does not expect the same level of service as one that makes a large purchase or frequent purchases.

2. **Price:** The cost of everything we purchase is becoming more and more important since people want to use their financial resources as efficiently as possible.

3. **Quality:** Customers want the products that they purchase to be durable and functional. Even perishable items should last long enough for them to be used without loss of value. Food items must be of a quality that does not endanger the health of the users. There is a psychological relationship between price and quality. Most customers consider it fair for companies to charge relatively higher prices for items deemed to be of superior quality than similar items from competitors.

4. **Action:** Customers are human beings and like to think that they are as important as any other person. They, therefore, expect action when a problem or question arises, i.e. someone will be ready to assist them when a problem arises.

5. **Appreciation:** Customers need to know that the employees of the companies from which they buy appreciate their money. Saying thank you to the customer through our words and actions is a good starting point.

Box 13-1

Your customers are your kings, queens, princes and princesses. They are also your employers. It is because of your customers that your businesses exist. They expect you to make them feel this way. If any of your key customers defects to a competitor, he leaves with a chain of others; if he remains, he brings in a chain of other customers.

— John Kuada and Madei Mangori

Market Orientation and Blue Ocean Strategy

These expectations must be fulfilled by a market-oriented company and its employees. As indicated in the introduction to this chapter, market-oriented companies are those that are highly sensitive to the needs of their customers and proactively take steps to fulfil these needs. Market-oriented companies have other defining characteristics (Kuada, 2016). First, they are capable of responding quickly to competitor challenges and are able to spot any evidence of customer dissatisfaction. Second, they are also able to quickly detect changes in customer needs and product preferences and take the necessary actions in response to the information. Third, they are also effective in getting all business functions to work together to provide superior customer value.

In 2005, W. Chan Kim and Renée Mauborgne from INSEAD published the book *Blue Ocean Strategy – How to Create Uncontested Market Space and Make Competition Irrelevant*. It quickly became a best seller because it provided a new strategic direction to many managers. They also popularised the concept of value innovation in that publication. Their argument is that market orientation alone cannot guarantee business success and growth. They describe those companies that strive to succeed in existing market space as adopting "red ocean" strategies, i.e. they serve an existing demand. In contrast, the more successful companies adopt "blue ocean" strategies. In blue oceans, demand is created rather than fought over, and there is ample opportunity for growth.

Kim and Mauborgne offer the following guidelines to companies in the blue ocean strategy formulation process:

1. **Do not** compete in existing market space, **instead** you should create uncontested market space.

2. **Do not** beat the competition, **instead** you should make the competition irrelevant.

3. **Do not** exploit existing demand, **instead** you should create and capture new demand.

4. **Do not** make the value/cost trade-off, **instead** you should break the value/cost trade-off.

5. **Do not** align the whole system of a company's activities with its strategic choice of differentiation or low cost, **instead** you should align the whole system of a company's activities in pursuit of both differentiation and low cost.

The Role of Employees in Making Customers Happy

As hinted earlier, it is the frontline employees that influence customers' perceptions of a service company's responsiveness to their needs. They do so through their personal willingness to go the 'extra mile' to serve their customers (or annoy them with their bad work attitude). This means that whether or not a customer perceives a company as delivering the service promised depends on the attitude, commitment and behaviour of service employees. The management literature shows that work attitude is partly shaped by organisational culture (Kuada and Hinson, 2014). This means a customer service environment should have a customer service-oriented culture.

Managing Customer Complaints

Managers must expect occasional mistakes in the service delivery process of their companies, no matter how well their employees try. A customer may accidentally be overcharged for service, there may be power outage, inputs suppliers may disappoint or a frontline employee may have a bad day. Customer complaint is, therefore, not entirely avoidable. As a service provider, it is the company's responsibility to respond to the customer's complaints in a manner that increases satisfaction. Even though complaints may sometimes seem undesirable, they nevertheless serve as a source of important feedback for the company. They contain the direct voice of the customer. If complaints are transformed into knowledge about customers, they can provide a valuable amount of goodwill for the company. A bank teller, for example, has no business snapping at a customer if the customer complains about the long wait s/he has had to endure before s/he was served. The customer's complaint is a free message to the bank that service might be too slow and customers may be uncomfortable about it. Complaining customers could be the most loyal customers of a company, if their complaints are well handled. A company must, therefore, design, build, operate and continuously upgrade systems for managing complaints. These systems are called customer complaint management systems (CCMS).

CHAPTER FOURTEEN

Financial Health Assessment

Managing business finances is important for creating a stable financial future for every company. This entails ensuring accurate financial recordkeeping. However, as many small business owners struggle to maintain balance in the midst of a hectic schedule, financial recordkeeping tasks often fall by the wayside and this can create serious cash flow problems for small companies. Hiring an experienced bookkeeper takes the burden off a sole proprietor. Business owners who adopt this option should make sure that they give their bookkeepers all relevant information to enable him or her maintain accurate records. It is also prudent for business owners to have some basic knowledge of the key financial records that are necessary to sustain the financial health of their small and growing companies. This chapter provides definitions and general knowledge of the essential financial indicators. Such knowledge will help business owners to interpret and self-audit records prepared by their accounting staff. Consistently self-auditing will determine whether accounting officers falsify records to cover up past mistakes or lapses in record keeping.

Some Important Financial Statements

The three most important financial statements that need to receive the attention of any owner of a small business are the balance sheet, income statement and cash flow statement. Without these financial statements, business owners will be blind to the financial health of the business.

Balance Sheet

The balance sheet of a business essentially identifies its net worth. With this statement, the company can identify whether the assets of the business exceeded its liabilities. This helps business owners to get a snapshot of their companies' health by indicating how much a company owns (its assets) and how much it owes (its liabilities).

Income Statement

The performance of a business is reflected in the income statement. There are generally two sections in the income statement: the operating and non-operating sections. The operating items section include revenues and expenses that are directly assignable to specific activities undertaken, for example, raw materials bought, salaries paid, goods and services sold. The non-operating items section discloses revenue and expense information about activities that are not tied directly to the company's regular operations.

Cash Flow Statement

The cash flow statement informs the business owners of their net income minus expenses over a given period. It, therefore, reflects how much free cash their businesses have to pay recurring expenses such as wages and salaries. This means they need to forecast and plan for the cash coming in and going out as accurately as possible.

Budgeting and Profitability

Business owners also need to request their accounting staff to prepare various budgets to guide operations. Budgets serve as financial plans of action for managers. They also help them to compare the financial health of their companies from one period to the other. Even small businesses must plan their budgets to ensure their operations stay on track. The budget process involves assessing all of the financial needs of a business and creating a financial road map for the business. Businesses that do not take budgeting seriously run the risk of underestimating earnings, which can ultimately lead to business failure.

Sales Budget

Sales budget is a forecast of revenue and expenses over a specified future period that establishes the expectations managers have about future earnings within a specific period. A more accurate sales forecast means better utilisation of resources, higher profitability and less wastage. It contains different elements, depending on how a business is organised. First, the company needs to estimate the demand for its goods and services in the market at given prices, and how much it is likely to sell based on a given set of marketing efforts and how much such marketing efforts are likely to cost the company. This is normally referred to as sales forecasting. The company may choose to consolidate these forecasts every month or for every quarter. The formula is simple and can be stated as follows:

Budgeted sales unit x budgeted sales price = Budgeted sales revenue.

A good starting point for such a budget is to go through the sales record for the previous period. For example, the amount of sales the company has been able to record in the previous year or quarter will act as a base to forecast what to expect in the next year or period. Of course, the planners need to take into account changes within the economy that can affect demand and internal conditions within the company that can influence production and costs. The accuracy of the forecasts will be greatly improved if the salespeople in the company are able to analyse customers' buying habits and intentions. This means they should talk to some of the key customers of the company and ground their estimates on the information they receive from them.

Profit Margin

It is also useful for business owners to have an understanding of the profitability of the goods and services they offer. One of the indicators of profitability is the profit margin. In simple terms, this is the percentage of selling price that is turned into profit, that is, what is left for the business after all operational costs are covered when a particular unit of goods or services are sold to a customer. Thus, profit is calculated by deducting direct costs, such as materials and labour and indirect costs (also known as overheads) from sales.

Business owners need to concern themselves with two types of profit margin:

1. gross profit margin; and
2. net profit margin.

Gross profit is calculated by subtracting total expenses from total revenue. That is,

Total revenue – total expenses = profit

To find the gross margin, divide the gross profit by the revenue. To make the margin a percentage, multiply the result by 100. The gross profit does not consider overhead expenses and, therefore, does not reveal the profitability of the entire business. To find this, we need to calculate the net profit (and then the net profit margin). This means we need to look at the profit after all expenses are deducted from the gross income (i.e. the company's net income) and divide that by the total sales, and then multiply the result by 100 to get the answer expressed as a percentage. Let us say the gross sales are $250,000 and expenses are $150,000. That means the net income is $100,000. Divide that number into gross sales (i.e. $100,000 divided by $250,000, = .40 X 100 = 40). It means the net profit margin equals 40%. A good margin will vary considerably by industry; but as a general rule of thumb, a 10% net profit margin is considered average, a 20% margin is considered high (or "good"), and a 5% margin is low.

Break-even Analysis

Another important financial analysis that tells the business owner whether the business will be successful is the break-even analysis. This analysis informs the business owner as to how many sales it takes to pay for the cost of doing business. In other words, how many of the goods and services provided should customers be willing to buy and pay for before it will make sense to engage in the business? This means the break-even point refers to the amount of revenue necessary to cover the total fixed and variable costs incurred by a company within a specified period.

A company can calculate its break-even quantity by using the formula below:

Break even quantity = Fixed costs / (Sales price per unit – Variable cost per unit)

Where:

1. Fixed costs are costs that do not change with varying output (e.g., salary, rent, building machinery).
2. Sales price per unit is the selling price (unit selling price) per unit.
3. Variable cost per unit is the variable costs incurred to create a unit.

Small business owners can use the calculation to determine how many product units they need to sell at a given price to break even, i.e. making neither losses nor profits. This means the business makes profit when sales are over the break-even point and losses when sales are less than the break-even point.

Accounts Payable

Accounts payable are the expenses a business pays to cover its operating costs. Without a proper accounting system in place, accounts may be paid late or not paid at all. Failing to pay one's expenses may be costly in both the short and long run. In the short run, the company may be required to pay penalties for the delay; it may also experience product delivery stop or utilities (such as electricity and water) turned off. In the long run, the company's suppliers may lose trust in it and, therefore, decide not to do business with the company.

Accounts Receivable

Account receivable are amounts that other people owe the company, i.e. what clients and customers are expected to pay. For small businesses with small profit margins, delays in receiving amounts that others owe may create serious cash flow problems. It is, therefore, important for these companies to keep track of how many days it takes the company to get its money back. Business owners should, therefore, require their accounting staff to calculate average debt collection periods. The smaller the average collection period is, the better it is for the company. However, companies must be aware that if their debt collection processes become stricter than those of their competitors, they can end up turning some customers away.

The average collection period is calculated by dividing a company's yearly accounts receivable balance by its yearly total net sales; this number is then multiplied by 365 to generate a number in days. The formula is shown below:

$$\text{Average Collection Period} = \frac{\text{Accounts Receivable Balance}}{\text{Total Net Sales}} \times 365$$

Net Working Capital

Another financial index that small business owners must pay attention to is the net working capital, which indicates the company's liquidity level, that is, its ability to meet short-term obligations and fund operations of the business. In simple terms, the net working capital is the difference between a company's current assets such as cash, accounts receivables and inventories on the one side and its current liabilities – accounts payables – on the other side.

Businesses must strive to have substantially positive net working capital figures, that is, they must have sufficient funds to cover their current liabilities. Substantially negative net working capital figures signal danger and possible bankruptcy. It is, therefore, important for business owners to undertake the trend analysis of their net working capital.

Current Ratio

In order to reduce the dangers of bankruptcy, business owners must keep keen eyes on their current assets and liabilities. A useful indicator of that is to calculate the company's current ratio. The current ratio is calculated by dividing the current assets of the business by the current liabilities. Potential creditors use the current ratio to measure a company's liquidity or ability to pay off short-term debts. A good current ratio is between 1.2 and 2, which means that the business has two times more current assets (than liabilities) to cover its debts. A current ratio below 1 means that the company doesn't have enough liquid assets to cover its short-term liabilities.

In addition to keeping an eye on its liquidity (ability to pay short-term obligations), businesses must also watch their solvency closely. Solvency is the ability of a company to meet its long-term obligations. This is measured using what is referred to as the solvency ratio. To calculate the ratio, divide a company's after tax net income by the sum of its liabilities (short-term and long-term). The lower a company's solvency ratio, the greater the probability that the company will default on its debt obligations. As a general rule of thumb, a solvency ratio of greater than 20% is considered financially healthy. With a lower solvency ratio, businesses will have to intensify their sales and marketing efforts in order to increase revenue in the medium or long term or increase profitability or sell some assets if market conditions for these assets are good. Alternatively, the company may have to increase owner equity, that is, the owner increases his investments in the company.

Overall Efficiency

Businesses are assessed to be efficient if they can generate substantial revenue with the assets that they have. This is also referred to as the business's rate of asset utilisation. Thus, the asset utilisation ratio (or asset turnover ratio) calculates the total revenue the company earns for every dollar of assets the company owns. In other words, increasing asset utilisation means the company is being more efficient with each dollar of assets it has. An asset turnover ratio of 6.5 means for every single dollar of asset the company is able to earn 6.5 dollars. If the asset utilisation increases over time, the company will be assessed as being run efficiently. It is important to note that when a business is expanding and therefore acquires new assets, its asset turnover ratio is likely to fall in the immediate following years since it takes time for assets to be employed in production of goods and services and for these products to generate revenue. Thus, the asset turnover ratio must be followed over time to determine the degree of efficiency of the company.

The Net worth of a Business

Finally, a business owner will be interested in knowing the net worth of the business; that is, how much he is likely to receive in dollars if the company is to be liquidated today and all debt obligations are covered. This provides a useful snapshot of the company's current financial position. A negative net worth means that there are more liabilities than assets in the company. Naturally, the business owner will strive to expand the net worth of the business. All the metrics noted above will help the business owner to constantly assess the extent to which the business is generating value for him.

Part 2
Profiles of Successful African Entrepreneurs

The Story of Mr Thatayaone Dichaba

Mr Thatayaone Dichaba

I hold a diploma in Computer Science. In 1998, when I was in university, I read a book _Rich Dad, Poor Dad_ by Robert Kiyosaki. When I finished reading the book, I knew deep inside that I was an entrepreneur; but in those days, the expectation and pressure to complete university and look for a job was a norm. So, I looked for a job at my friend's company as a website developer. I was literally doing everything in the company – marketing, accounting, sales and management. It was a start-up company and the feeling of learning everything was overwhelming and that was exactly what I wanted. Two years later, I went on my own entrepreneurial journey. I started a computer networking company, and used to walk under the scorching heat, knocking on business doors and doing sales with my business partner who later became my wife. She handled all administrative work. The business did quite well.

I have always believed that the first capital I have, which to me is very tangible, is my integrity. When I started, I used whatever profits I made from my business then to kick-start my dreams. I approached Citizen Entrepreneurial Development Authority (CEDA) for a loan. Later on, I had some friends who lent me some money because of my integrity. I struggled with finances but never with capital. I believe that if I still have my integrity, I can attract finances, and I still do actually.

I love dreaming. I started having dreams and ambitions when I was much younger. I never stopped dreaming. Dreams is what keeps propelling me. Today, I am where I was dreaming when I was much younger, though I must admit that it took me over 16 years to realise some dreams. I love dreaming to the extent that one of my businesses uses a slogan "Dream it". I continuously keep an image of where and how I want to solve challenges within my sphere of influence on the canvas of my imagination. I keep refining this image every now and then. It keeps getting better as I go on to GET IT DONE. The dream is also written in my journals, imprinted in my office and even in my personal resting place (bedroom). This is how serious I take my dreams.

However, the truth is that I have had more failures than successes. I mean so far. In the early 2000, when being attached by a Deputy Sheriff was like a taboo in our society, and being published in local newspapers in the section of, in-the-matter-between, I had quite a lot of failures. I had my assets listed for sale. I received a lot of calls from friends and concerned family members as this was a public shame. I refused to give up. Most reputable deputy sheriffs in town have had opportunity to either attach my assets or serve me. Some are now my friends. My position remains the same. I grew up in a small village where we used to herd cattle. There were some aggressive dogs that would bark at a bull or attempt to attack it, especially a big bull with horns. However, the smart ones would not dare come closer. They knew what could happen, hence a saying in my language "Ntsa di bogola Poo", translated "Dogs are barking at a bull". That's how I see failure. Learn from it and be bold. Be like a bull to failure. As long as you learn from it, you can attack your failures easily. I have had major losses. I carry many scars, being sometimes misunderstood.

When I started business, it was and is my inspiration to start building businesses that can grow and create opportunities for others, but I learned along the way that not only did I start building businesses, but businesses started building me. In the beginning, I used to wonder why I stayed small. Why do we have many small businesses and never have conglomerates and unicorns or corporate giants. Strive Masiyiwa said that the reason was simply because of "structure." I gave a lot of thought to it and then I engaged consultants to come evaluate why I was not growing. I hearkened to Strive's advice. African entrepreneurs must understand that big businesses are big by intention. The fact that you started a business doesn't mean you are the right person to manage it. Reflect, and recognise your strengths and weaknesses. Get others to mitigate your weaknesses.

There is a lot of wisdom in the saying that lack of growth is a sign that stagnation and death could be looming. One has to continuously innovate around the circumstances one finds oneself in. Management problems can be the reason small business stay small. Ask yourself as the leader of your business, are you the stumbling block to its growth? Has it outgrown you? Think soberly about these indicators and make the right decisions to grow. Sometimes, experience is overrated and can be a stumbling block to exploring the unknown and new possibilities. So, create a balance between experience and the quest to explore unknown territories. To succeed, you must plan, learn and implement, and keep repeating until you see results.

If you are looking for external finances in order to grow, remember that investors invest not only in viable and scalable businesses but also in the leader. So, character plays a pivotal role. Character can trigger investor's confidence or kill it. Your leadership style is also important. My readings have taught me that a leader must motivate those around him to maximise their God-given gifts and potential. Our Maker is so generous, in that He has given all of us gifts. The responsibility of leaders is to help others maximise their potential. Thus, it gives me joy when those around me discover their true potential and work towards maximising it.

I believe in lifelong learning. I am currently doing a Stanford Seed Programme, and I am loving it, learning how to structure and grow business, and interacting with other entrepreneurs, because entrepreneurship is lonely. I read many business books. I am inspired by reading about others who have walked before me or after me who are doing great things. One man said, "If you read the highest thoughts of uncommon man, you will have their experience." Some of my favourite authors include Dr Myles Munroe, Peter Jakes Daniel, an Australian entrepreneur and author. I also read books by Brian Tracy, Stephen R Covey, and Jack Welch.

Another important source of knowledge for me is listening to audio and video on YouTube of inspiring authors and the life stories of other known entrepreneurs. Some of them are R. G. LeTourneau: Mover of Men and Mountains – an American inventor / businessman, Strive Masiyiwa – Zimbabwe born entrepreneur, Richard Branson and Elon Musk. I am also inspired by Dr E. A. Sitima – my mentor/ coach who taught me how to lead by Motivation and Wisdom. In addition to these sources of inspiration, I attend leadership workshops/seminars and travel to other places for benchmarking and learning. I have been to Mauritius, Ghana, Kenya, Mozambique, DRC, Zambia, Zimbabwe, Namibia, Angola, South Africa, Spain, Uganda, England, Bahrain, Dubai and China, on business.

Above all, my spirituality is the pinnacle of my entire being. Holding on to the Biblical principles of success that I adhere to, has given me the stability and helped me to anchor my faith in my dreams and purpose. In times of difficulties and stress, I pray, meditate and take off some time to reflect and I always ask myself questions, why am I stressed? What can I do to change that? If it's beyond my control, wait in faith. In the past, I stressed, worried, and feared about things that never happened. There is power in positive thinking.

So far, I have pushed myself hard, and I am still on the journey. It is good to see our customers happy and using our products and technologies. My assessment today is that we are on the right course. We have represented Botswana quite well, especially brand Botswana as some of our companies export to other countries within the African region. We have pioneered some industries that were otherwise known to be only possible in developed countries, such as manufacturing of electronic gadgets and setting up assembly plants. There is a lot that needs to be done. The business is privately owned and it is valued at over US$25 million.

The Story of Mr Peter Cunningham

Mr Peter Cunningham
Chief Executive Officer (CEO) of Hamara Group of Companies

My name is Peter Cunningham. I am the current CEO of Hamara Group of Companies, which is, we believe, one of the most exciting groups of companies for unlocking the agricultural potential of Africa.

Our vision statement is to "unlock the productive potential of Africa." We believe that this potential is in small-scale farmers and so we are a company that is centred around creating value chains in chickens, poultry, dairy, nuts and tree crops where we provide inputs and we buy back products from farmers. The world is increasingly short of food and with many forces of urbanisation, climate change, changing food footprints, genetic modification potential plateauing, etc. Into this, the small-scale farmers of sub-Saharan Africa are the future answer for this. This is very exciting and we believe that there is productive, personal and business potential in this.

I was born in 1967 to a fantastic family who were not very wealthy but an immense sense of vision, purpose and values. I decided when I was 7 years old that I wanted to be a farmer. My mother at the time said to me that unfortunately, we needed money to be a farmer and as a family, we did not have that kind of money. I explained to her that she had told us since we were born that, if Jesus was with us, He could do things. She then gave me 50 day-old chicks for my 8th birthday. I then raised them, sold them and bought 60, raised them, sold them and bought 75 and continued to grow until when I finished school, I was doing 10 000 chickens a time.

I then did a poultry science degree at Edinburgh University for three years and, when I came back, started ostrich farming. It was during this time that I really felt a sense of connection with Jesus and with the spiritual world. Up until then, I had always questioned why it was that if it was true that Jesus really loved us, then there was no real relationship. I had always been sceptical about the hypocrisy that I saw in so much of the church and in myself where we say that Jesus loves us, died for us, he is the King of the Universe and yet when we come to pray, it is like we are praying to a ceiling or to something that does not exist. I had always battled with that. I managed to get asked to leave three churches as a result of this questioning.

> "Correct worldview, mindset, vision, business purpose and commitment for the long haul are keys to the creation of worthwhile businesses in Africa"
>
> *Mr Peter Cunningham CEO of Hamara Group of Companies*

However, right from the outset of starting the business, we began to feel and see amazing miracles happen. This resulted in us ending up with one of the largest ostrich businesses in Zimbabwe and subsequently in Africa. I married my wife Diana in 1992 and that was the infamous 1992 drought where we had one tenth of our normal rainfall. The business was virtually going into liquidation within two months of being married.

We managed to get a contract in Northern Zimbabwe to supply ostriches. We literally drove 21 days night and day, i.e. driving 12 hours there to deliver ostriches during the day and 12 hours back at night to load the next group to go the following day and that was the foundation of how we started our marriage. After that, we got through 1992 and the business started to grow significantly.

In 1996, we were putting a percentage of our profits for helping the poor and the more vulnerable and I remember the day my older brother who was working with me at the time came and said that we have got all this all wrong. We are looking at this as if Africa is a poor continent with poor people and we are helping them out. His view was that actually we need to relook at Africa as the richest continent with the richest people and we need to help them to see their potential and unlock the resources they have both in themselves and the land that is around them. That led to some revolutionary six months of discussions. We ended up recalibrating our business from a farming business to an agricultural value chain business incorporating small-scale farmers as initially contractors where we provided day-old chicks and feeds and then bought back the birds. This was extremely successful and it led to us growing significantly as a business.

In 2000, we then diversified this model from ostriches to chickens and immediately hit all of the snags one could hit. However, with ostriches, we were the only supplier of chicks and the only buyer of birds, with chickens everybody could eat them, everybody needed them and the food could be sold easily and so we immediately hit all the normal problems that one could hit with side marketing. This led to two to three years of intense grappling both as a family and as a business because we had seen the raw potential of unlocking the entrepreneurial drive and spirit of small-scale farmers and realised that this really has the power to change Africa.

However, without a change of character and without a change of world view where a poverty mindset prevailed, they would grab everything that they could. This is reinforced by many good intentioned projects and aid initiatives which led to a project mindset that sees people as a project and leaves communities feeling that this is going to come and go and so and take what they can. It took two years of intense battling through this until in 2004. We started to do a lot of pastoral training and conferences because we felt that it was through the church that we could do this and that ended up being an epic failure as well.

We discovered that many church leaders unfortunately are more interested in their Sunday services and in themselves than their people and became quite disillusioned with the potential of the church to change Africa. Not all of it because there are some good people but many have the traditional ways of doing church.

It was around this time that we started to be challenged that the future of Africa and the future of farming was actually in the hands of the youth. However, we saw that younger people, as soon as they became anything or started in life, wanted to get to town and get out of the rural areas and farming. Farming was kind of the position you had after you had failed in everything else. At the same time, 70% of Africa is under 26 and 50% of Zimbabweans are under the age of 18, with the average age of a Zimbabwean being 18.

We started to see that, actually, the mindset we need to change was not the older people which we were battling with, but to help the youth to see that they could create a whole new future in themselves, their families, in farming and business, and that they could be wealth creators rather than job takers. This led us to start the Ebenezer Agricultural College in 2006 which got underway properly in 2007.

Ebenezer is an agricultural college which takes young men and ladies for two years. They are given their own farms or portions of the farms. They earn graduation rewards. They work those portions of the farms and share in the profit of what they earn for the period that they are there.

They also do three hours of academic studies daily. This is one hour on vision and life skills and what we are really living for; one hour on business, cash transfers, budgets, contracts, etc., and one hour on animal and crop husbandry. This started a spark what has been revolutionary in our lives as well as in the lives of the students. We saw the immense change and potential of people who found purpose, destiny and hope that the future of Africa is actually in farming and is in raw production and at a later stage once that reaches fulfilment that industrialisation and other stuff will follow. These graduates became model farmers. What we have seen and known throughout Africa is that models are exciting and easy to copy. However, if you tell somebody they can do something, it is harder for them to conceptualise it or believe it; but if they see it in somebody else, it becomes a natural thing to feel that they could do, i.e. they could become that kind of person. So, with pointing to these model farmers, we were able to do a massive mobilisation effort which we started in 2012. This involved mobilising communities, churches and others to see the potential inherent in Africa and Zimbabwe. Instead of being pushed into community development, it was now pull as people could see the vision and see what they could be and do. This led to the creation of TMG which drives that department.

This developed a training staff and programme of over 30 amazing people and trained over 15,000 farmers in the following years. We then opened another division on creating capacity to give technical backup and support. We were providing the day-old chicks, feed, seedlings, fertilisers, chemicals, etc. and buying back the product. This model has grown from strength to strength since then.

One day, I was reading the FAO report about the world food crisis. It was talking about genetic modification reaching its peak, climate change with urbanisation, etc. that population growth, changing food footprint of China, which is eating more meat products that the world was going to face increasing food crisis and that the only hope was going to come from sub-Saharan Africa. However, it pointed out that this is in the hands of the small-scale farmers who are less productive and, therefore, the world could not look at them with much hope. This made me feel very excited because this is our exact model. We believe that the small-scale farmers of Africa can be even more efficient than any large producers and that we have proved this and that we are on a journey to expanding production. So, that is where we are today. Our company runs feed mills, breed farms, hatcheries, outgrower programmes and buys back its product for both local and export consumption. The heart of it is the training and mentoring programmes around Ebenezer, TMG and Africa Alive which is catalysing the vision, hope and capacity that is in our people.

Today, Sondelani is a company with a vision to release the productive potential of Africa. We believe the power of Africa is in her people who have enormous potential, most of whom are small-scale farmers who live in naturally productive areas. Sondelani has deep roots in agriculture (and more specifically, small-scale farming) but now has branches in food processing and retail, all held together by the sturdy trunk of well-developed value chains that ensure the success of our small-scale farmer partners. Our flagship brand, Hamara (meaning ours), is built on the premise that production is done by "all of us together." We put together agricultural value chains and provide total solutions and inputs for farmers and we provide horticultural, poultry and dairy products from farmers – in other words, a complete value chain from inputs to markets. Our unique set-up sees us being one of a handful of licensed Broiler and Layer breeders in the country; we operate state-of-the-art hatcheries and also run a top-notch feed mill, being the only company in the country that produces day-old chicks and commercial animal feeds in-house. We also operate one of the only two tomato processing plants in the country, having recently commissioned a state-of-the-art facility in Bulawayo that has the capacity to process 150 tons of tomatoes per day of operation, providing quality tomato paste for local and regional industrial consumption and a reliable off-take for local farmers. Our Hamara Dairy is also producing quality products for the local market, including our popular amasi, yoghurt, butter and fresh milk (courtesy of our pedigree Jersey herd) while the Hamara Egg brand is Matabeleland's most established egg brand. We have trained 15000 small-scale farmers through TMG (originally Turning Matabeleland Green), a non-profit organisation that seeks to develop a network of competent farmer partners to meet the country's growing food and export needs. We also run Ebenezer Training Centre, an agricultural college for the youth; the college develops skilled farmers through a sought-after two-year on-site diploma programme. The business is privately owned and turns over US$24 million per year from a total initial capital input of 50 day-old broiler chickens.

We had numerous massive failures and one of them is being overexposed on borrowing, in 2008. This is when Zimbabwe got into free fall. We had massive challenges that nearly brought the company down. We created a policy of not trying to borrow apart from collateral management stock. We have also done many partnerships and realised that these will only work when partners have truly the same values and vision and that making money as a primary purpose is seldom a recipe on which long-term partnerships can be built.

On the question of foundations for success across Africa and advice I would give to new entrepreneurs and business people, I would say two things. Firstly, a lot of people have the 'get-rich-quick' mentality and my feeling is that worthwhile businesses are built over time. People need to be committed to the long haul that growing slowly and solidly ends up with the best results. People take on too much debt, try to do more than the capacity they have to do well at that time and then end up struggling. I think the second thing is that I believe businesses can grow best if they have a real purpose apart from purely making money for the owner. If we can connect with the vision that Africa can be and the potential for Africa, I think we draw in a whole lot of skill sets, vision sets and the call to our people to be something that is bigger than themselves, and this creates an energy and capacity that can really move us. In this journey, I personally have come to know and relish Jesus life with us, not in a boring religious formality way, but in a living active relationship practically engaged with us in strategy, direction and execution.

The Story of Dr Collen Msasanure

Personal, Professional and Entrepreneurial Portrait

Dr Collen Msasanure

Dr Collen Msasanure is a consultant orthopaedic surgeon in both private and public practice. He is the head of orthopaedics at United Bulawayo Central Hospital, and President of the Zimbabwe Orthopaedic Association. He is also a lecturer at the National University of Science and Technology (NUST) Medical School as well as at the College of Surgeons of East Central and Southern Africa (ATLS). He also serves as instructor and administrative pastor at Celebration Church Bulawayo. Alongside all these areas of activity, Collen Msasanure is active in Zimbabwe Hospital and Prisons Care Ministry and helps manage

Sizolwethu (a mobile health clinic for the underprivileged) as well as Zimbabwe Orthopaedic Trust.

In terms of formal education, he holds university level qualification in medicine. He has a wide international exposure, travelling extensively within Africa, Europe and America on professional assignments.

Learning does not happen only formally or through continuous professional development but also through obtaining some degree of international exposure through international experience obtained through travel whether for leisure or business as well.

He described his dreams, ambitions and career journey as follows:

> Journey started early high school following an accident involving my father. I was inspired by how my mother handled it. I then decided that I was going to be a doctor in order to protect my family healthwise. When I started working, I never intended to go into business. My goal was to save lives and assist those that are underprivileged.

When the economy in Zimbabwe collapsed, I found myself having to think twice about going into medical business. Long and short of it, I opened a private practice. The practice evolved from a GP orthopaedic service to a specialist orthopaedic practice. This was followed by opening the first of its kind in the country, a surgical hospital: Bulawayo Surgical Hospital.

His initial source of inspiration was his mother, a nurse who unceasingly encouraged him to follow his dreams and ambitions in life. He frequently visited Botswana after his university education and worked there periodically to build a financial base for entering private medical practice. He explained the initial investment decisions as follows:

> I worked in neighbouring Botswana and saved up some money, partnered with my brother, Cephas Msasanure, and brother-in-law, Madei Mangori and later my friend and colleague Munyaradzi Magara. Put the little resource together (Grossly inadequate). Innovation found me befriending a UK-based company, which was in the business of salvaging laid off equipment and refurbishing it. This gave us mileage in acquiring equipment. Continued to work whilst setting up and raising more money and importing refurbished equipment. After one year of set-up, paying employees, and rentals we were licensed. In terms of non-financial resources, I received a lot of support from my wife,

Mercy Msasanure, our pastor Dr Tawafadza Makoni, Pastor Tom Deuschle, the team that I had employed and my family.

He has always been eager to adopt best practices within the industry by learning from others, especially those in other parts of the world. He explains:

> I visited a friend in the USA and spent time shadowing his practice. When I came back, we moved my consulting room practice to a more suitable building and did a set-up equivalent to what I had learnt. We computerised the records and went paperless, improved the ambience and outlook of the practice, made the working environment friendly. This turned our practice around. Our patient flow improved; revenue flows improved. We operated more patients. On the other hand, in the Surgical Hospital, we were able to improve the equipment by buying newer and more equipment.

Doing business successfully within the Zimbabwean environment has its own unique challenges, especially due to the turbulent political circumstances.

> In Zimbabwe, the target is a moving target and have to re-evaluate one's strategy every minute," he explains and continues, "We found ourselves moving from office to office and court to court after being dragged to the labour court for not following the National Employment Council (NEC) and labour remuneration regulations. Learnt it the hard way. Like any other health institution, we experienced patient complications that taught us valuable lessons.

Dr Collen Msasanure is a highly inspired man. He has many sources of inspiration that gives him joy in life despite life challenges. He has deliberate plans to cope with stress. This includes his involvement in non-profit activities, fellowship at his church, praying, gardening, exercising, spending time and doing things together with his family.

He has the following words of advice for other African entrepreneurs:

1. If you want to run a successful, long-lasting business, you must own the property you are running the business from.
2. Invest in learning from the experiences of those who have gone before you, copy and improve. Invest in consultation. Learn and try out new ways of doing business.

The Story of Mr Davidson Norupiri

Looking at the world through new lenses

Mr Davidson Norupiri

Mr Davidson Norupiri is the Founder and Managing Director of Davipel Trading, a privately owned company based in Zimbabwe. The company manufactures a wide range of dried foods, most of which are maize by-products. Davipel Group of companies is wholly owned by Mr D. and Mrs P. Norupiri, who are also the company's founders and directors. The company was established in 2002 with the objective of supplying quality dried foods to both the local market and export market. According to *The Herald* of 24 June 2020, the group invested US$12 million in snack plants. Asked in an interview recently about Davipel, Mr Davidson Norupiri stated:

We have invested into the whole value chain system as far as food processing is concerned. So, knowing that we are an agro-based economy, we have a strong bias towards maize products. We invested in a milling plant for us to be able to supply ourselves in some of our production factories. So, we have got the milling plant which we call Agri-Milling. This milling plant feeds into our other two subsidiaries.

The first subsidiary is the Snack Division, which is a manufacturing plant for corn snacks. We also have a separate subsidiary called Flavouroom, which processes and packages other by-products like instant porridge, samp, beer powder and soya chunks. Both subsidiaries take their core raw materials from the Agri-Milling plant. Our value chain is anchored around adding value to maize. We buy maize locally from GMB (i.e. Grain Marketing Board) – which means we are supporting the local maize farmers with guaranteed market offtake. We also use a lot of oil, sourced from local oil companies. We use 25 000 litres of oil a day to fry our snacks.

Currently, we crush 216 tonnes of maize a day. The maize crushing process produces four (4) outputs – roller meal, refined mealie meal, grits, and bran. The grits is an essential input for our other plants as we further process it into by-products like snacks, instant porridge and powdered beverages. Bran, which is the cheapest component, is processed into stockfeed.

Most of the formulations that we are using are coming from as far as Switzerland. All this technology translates into job creation for the community, and knowledge transfer to our food technologists who also cascade the knowledge to our plant operators. To enhance our skills development, we have built a training facility, which we call a skills and technology transfer centre. The facility is well resourced with training technology convenient for our staff training.

We have also invested in very modern machinery; hence, we do not have any equipment which is more than 4 years old. All our equipment, our boiler included, is [are] environmentally friendly and none of them uses pollutant fuels like coal. To minimise dust that is emitted from the manufacturing of our flavours, we have invested in a comprehensive dust collection system that traps and disposes dust particles in a manner recommended by the national environment management authorities.

We try as much as we can to minimise pollution in all our processes. We are now working on the ISO 9000 Standard.

To minimise pilferage, we came up with a loss control department which is headed by a former police officer. The personnel is closely involved in the daily operations and has been quite resourceful in setting up systems that minimise risk and losses. We also try to pay our staff salaries which are slightly above the union recommendation, to keep them motivated and also reduce the temptation for pilferage.

About Davipel Trading

Davipel's quest for growth and viability is clearly defined in its vision and mission statements whose main emphasis is on offering unparalleled quality products for both local and export market. Customer satisfaction has been ensured at Davipel Trading by the streamlined processes which are in place as well as the dedicated employees, some of whom have been with the company since inception.

Being a well-established local manufacturer and product developer, matching and manufacturing lead times are extremely competitive when compared to other manufacturers. The flat reporting structure at Davipel Trading allows for speedy decision-making and the company is extremely flexible in production when it comes to adapting to its customer needs. The food technologists are in touch with local taste and preferences and can develop products which suit local segmented market taste and buying power.

The group has a freight services subsidiary with a fleet of trucks that serve the group's local deliveries while utilising alternative distribution networks to deliver to other parts of Zimbabwe and Southern Africa. They also have branches in Bulawayo and Mutare, to cater for the Matabeleland and Manicaland markets respectively.

Davipel Products

Davipel Trading products are traded under the brand names Jumbo, Sunny, Royal, Diggles, and Brewer's Pride.

Jumbo is the dominant brand for the range of corn snacks. The brand, which comes in a variety of flavours, has grown to be the market leader in the category, proving to be extremely popular with children. Other brands in the company's portfolio of snacks are Sunny Snacks and Diggles.

Other Davipel Products

The company also produces Royal Chunks, a popular brand of soya mince. The product offers value for money to the mass market, coming in 250g, 500g, 1kg and 4kg pack sizes. Other products within the Davipel product portfolio include instant porridge, beer powder, maheu powder, and samp. All these are maize by-products.

Over the years, the group has vertically integrated its operations throughout the whole maize supply chain, from maize crushing until the final packaged product is put on shelf. Hence, consumers always expect to get the best price. Mr Norupiri, in a function of officially opening the Davipel Group of companies in its new location, Sunway City Harare, stated: "We are the largest in Zimbabwe and third largest in the region which has 150 snack producing companies. Our ambition is to be recognised as the largest in the region." Mr Norupiri said the investment was a sign of their commitment to Zimbabwe. "This investment shows our commitment to Zimbabwe and is a response to the clarion call for investment to create jobs. This investment has created 400 jobs," he added.

The corn snack manufacturing plant was established in 2002, while the milling company Agri-Milling was established in 2018. Meanwhile Davipel donated 10 tonnes of mealie-meal to First Lady Auxillia Mnangagwa's charity, Angel of Hope.

The Story of Mr Chenjerai Tsuro

Mr Chenjerai Tsuro (Correct identity has been disguised for anonymity) is an equity partner as well as executive finance director and company secretary of XYZ Pvt Ltd (Correct identity has been disguised for anonymity) based in Harare, Zimbabwe. He was one of three key members in the relaunching of XYZ Pvt Ltd onto the market in October 2017, having been able to attract an equity partner into the business after the business had shut down for about five (5) years, and mothballing of the XYZ Pvt Ltd plant. The business exports and generates foreign currency running into millions of United States dollars. The business is in the agricultural sector and represented throughout the appropriate agricultural growing regions in the country.

The nature of Mr Tsuro's responsibilities in the company are as follows:

- As one of the shareholders and a key strategic business partner to the CEO and the organisation's leadership team, provides proactive financial support across the business.
- Oversees the financial and accounting management, internal and external reporting, and treasury functions.
- Ensures efficient and accurate financial forecasting, management reporting, and planning systems are in place. Supports the CEO in the preparation of realistic operating budgets. Co-ordinates the ongoing financial analysis and risk management activities of the company's operations, interpreting and presenting relevant financial data to the CEO and the management team, and making appropriate recommendations.
- Develops and implements plans to optimise the company's capital structure and the financial strategies for the company's growth and development.
- Maintains and expands banking relationships to support market access in the company's future debt and equity sourcing activities.
- Works with the CEO in coordinating the strategic planning process to evaluate growth opportunities through joint ventures, acquisitions and internal expansion, as well as internal restructuring.

- Manages tax planning, reporting activities and maintaining liaison with service providers.
- Maintains a system of internal controls and audit procedures, including managing the company's relationship with its outside audit firm.
- As a member of the senior leadership team, contributes to decisions, which affect the enterprise as a whole.

In terms of formal education, he holds a Master of Business Leadership (MBL) obtained from the University of South Africa (UNISA) as well as a Bachelor of Accountancy Honours (Accountancy) from the University of Zimbabwe. Professionally, Mr Chenjerai Tsuro is a Fellow Chartered Secretary (FCIS) – Chartered Institute of Secretaries Zimbabwe, now known as the Chartered Institute of Governance.

Prior to starting XYZ Pvt Ltd, Mr Chenjerai Tsuro was a Tax Assessor in the Department of Taxes in Zimbabwe's Ministry of Finance where he was responsible for training of subordinates, assessing individuals, companies, partnerships, farmers and deceased estates. The beginnings of his professional career were fraught with some challenges. He recounted:

> When the results for my last year at university came, I had to sit for a supplementary exam in one of subjects which resulted in me not getting an articled clerk position to become a chartered accountant through one of the big four accounting firms being turned down. I tried to explain to the partners then that I was going to re-sit and pass the exam, but they didn't believe me. The response devastated me as I had to rethink of a new career path and realised that I had to work very hard to prove to myself that I was not a failure. I sat for the supplementary exam, passed and graduated with my year class. I had to start looking for a job and started at the Department of Taxes as a Tax Assessor. I knew then that I was not going to stay for long in any particular job until I got what I wanted to do. Some of the lessons I learnt are never, ever to give up on one's dream, patience, persistence and pray (what I call the three Ps). The death of my parents who passed on eight months after each other, immediately after I got married taught me to grow up very fast as a man. I had to learn to look after a wife, my two siblings, one of whom was alcoholic and be head of a family, being the second born in a family of five.

Asked about his early motivation triggers and how he started on his entrepreneurial career journey, Mr Chenjerai Tsuro responded as follows:

> I was working for a company in the motor industry as a Finance Manager and I had played a major role in the turnaround of the business. I asked to be promoted to be a Finance Director and participate in the profits of the business. From the time I made the request, my relationship with my Managing Director then soured and I had to look for a way out amicably. My break came when I was invited to join a company that was under Administration by the State as a Finance Director in April 2006. I left a cosy job in a financial services company and took a big risk. The business was offered to management in about mid of 2006. The Managing Director and myself took up the challenge and we ran around to look for the money for a 100% buyout. I sold a vehicle I had bought for my wife and shares I had on the Zimbabwe Stock Exchange to invest in the company. My partner made similar contributions and we got some support from one of the financial institutions in Harare.

> What inspired me most to start this journey was the opportunity to work for myself and leave an inheritance for my children's children. I was also inspired by my partner, Mr Strive Masiyiwa- his tenacity not to give up. I also got a lot of psychological and spiritual support from my wife who encouraged me to pursue the dream of owning a business.

As his involvement in the business increased, Mr Tsuro was encouraged by his wife to enrol for an MBA programme in Leadership in order to upgrade his management skill for the business and to strengthen his capacity to manage various aspects of his private life. It was a four-year programme, which involved going away from home for at least twice a year. It required a lot of discipline and tenacity. Reflecting on that period in his life, he remarked:

> One lesson that I will never forget is a statement which was said by one of the professors on the course when he said "If you are 40 (forty) years today, in 4 (four) years' time you will be 44 (forty-four) years old whether you like it or not. But the decision you make today is, what you will be in four years' time - whether just being 44 years old and we celebrate and say happy birthday with a big cake and candles or we

celebrate being 44 years old with a Master in Business Leadership degree programme". Those words kept me going during the studies and the other lesson is that time does not stop for anyone. The choice to work and succeed is within one's control.

He still attends professional development conferences and seminars/workshops as a means of further improving his managerial capabilities and as a way of networking with people with similar ambitions and learning from their success stories and pitfalls in business. "One has to have a never-ending quest to learn to improve oneself to be a better person," he observes. He also draws immense professional inspiration from the Internet and follows 'Future Learn' online courses.

To him, learning does not happen only formally or through continuous professional development but also through obtaining some degree of international exposure through international experience obtained through travel whether for leisure or business. For this reason, Mr Chenjerai Tsuro enjoys travelling. He has travelled to regional countries such as Zambia and Malawi while working for an international energy company. He also travelled to Germany, Kenya and South Africa for business conferences. As for leisure travel, he has visited the following countries on family vacations over the years – United States of America, South Africa, Kenya, Mozambique, Thailand, Mauritius and The United Kingdom.

Mr Tsuro had some challenges in his personal life and these challenges have taught him useful lessons. He informs as follows:

> Before I got married, at the age of 26, I had secured a residential stand in one of the low-density suburbs and a bedsitter apartment in town, which was a big achievement as one of my dreams is to invest in real estate. After I got married, we started looking for a house and lost our low-density suburb stand due to miscommunication and misunderstanding when we had identified a completed house to purchase. We lost the stand and did not buy the house. I was disappointed, but life had to continue and we secured another residential stand. There is power in agreement and good communication. We did not give up. About 10 years later, we were back in the first low density suburb where we had lost a stand through purchasing a completed house.

He is very proud of his achievements so far. He takes special pride in being involved in the turnaround of XYZ Company in 2006. However, his greatest joy comes from being able to send their two children to the best schools even during difficult and challenging times. He is a very religious man and is guided in his daily life by the words of the Bible, especially Psalm 37: 25 which reads: *"I have been young and now I am old, but I have never seen the righteous forsaken nor their children begging for bread."*

Working in an unpredictable and volatile political and economic environment has also taught him a number of lessons of life. These include *never, never, never, ever to give up on one's dream, to be diligent, focusing on the main thing/dream so that one is not all over the place, appearing to be busy without achieving anything, working hard, being adaptable, changing with the times, not spending time mourning on one's past failures and keeping on dreaming.* Consistent with his *never, never, never, ever to give up on one's dream* philosophy, Mr Chenjerai Tsuro is a highly inspired man. He has many sources of inspiration. These give him joy in life despite what life throws at him and his family in the form of life challenges. He also has deliberate plans to cope with stress. He categorically stated that the Holy Bible is one of his favourite books for wisdom on life. He reads a chapter of the Book of Proverbs every day of every month. This means that he reads the Book of Proverbs 12 times in a year. In addition, he reads the whole Bible from Genesis to Revelation every year. Among his other favourite book authors are Robert Kiyosaki author of *Rich Dad, Poor Dad, The Cashflow Quadrant* as well as Dale Carnegie the author of *How to Win Friends and Influence People.*

On coping with stress, Mr Tsuro indicated that he does morning daily Bible devotions with family and personally exercises every day through walking about 4.2 km daily for five days of the week. He also eats healthy, sleeps well, keeps short accounts with people, i.e. does not keep grudges, does not watch much news but keeps abreast of what is happening around him. He also indicated that he does not spend a lot of time on social media.

What gives him most joy in life personally and professionally is spending time with his family, going on family vacations and attending continuous professional development (CPD) courses / workshops. His most favourite management principles are planning – choosing appropriate goals; determining what strategies to use and what resources are needed to achieve the goals; organising; controlling that is evaluating how well one is achieving one's goals; improving performance; and taking actions.

In his view, some of the major weaknesses of most African entrepreneurs include their pursuit of instant gratification (i.e. not thinking about tomorrow), not taking care of the disadvantaged and vulnerable in society, placing excessive emphasis on material possessions rather than investing for tomorrow or creating resources for the younger generation. He advises as follows:

> Maintaining a good health and wellness which impacts on the physical, spiritual and mental is key in surviving through turbulent times, feeding one's mind with information that adds value to one's life, not spending too much time on negative energy, always telling the truth and the truth will set one free are critical for leaders. If one tells the truth, one does not have to remember anything because it's the truth. If one tells a lie, one has to keep on remembering the lies, one told before. One must keep on dreaming. If one stops dreaming, one will be dead. Above all, one must cultivate a culture of reading and continuous learning to keep one's mind busy and active.

Case Study Questions:

1. What do you consider the major strengths and weaknesses of Mr Chenjerai Tsuro as an entrepreneur and a manager?
2. What lessons can you learn from his story for your own entrepreneurial journey?

The Story of Mrs Edna Mukurazhizha

CEO of Empowered Woman Excel Savings and Credit Cooperative Society (SACCOs)

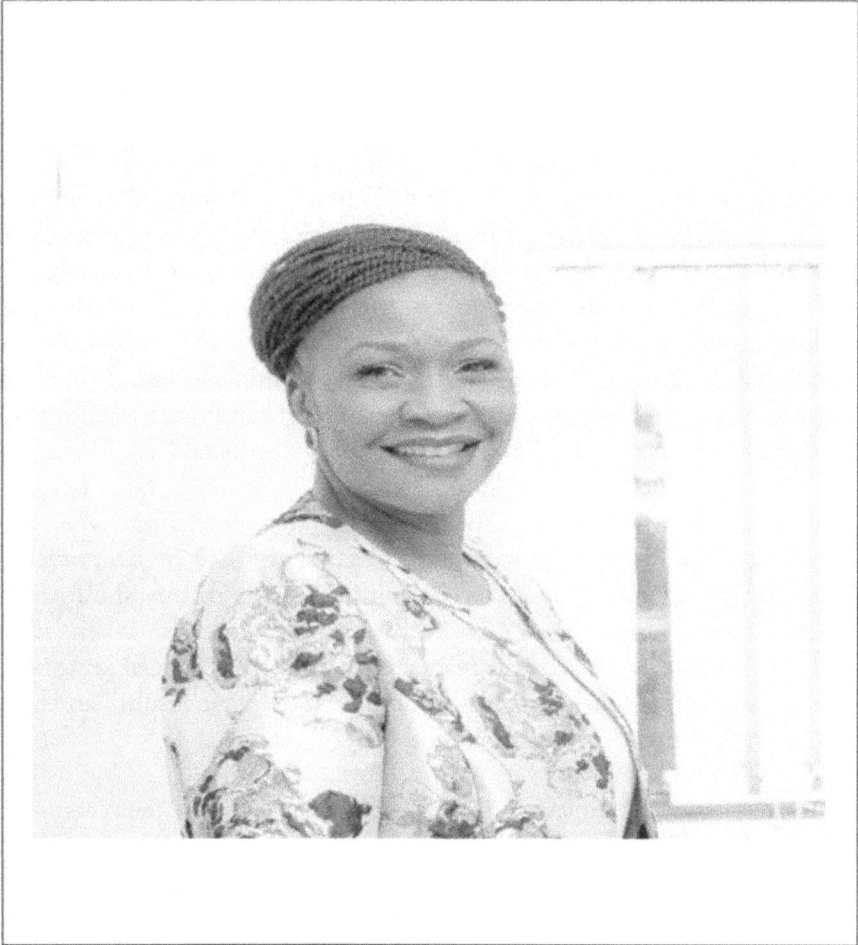

When you empower a woman, you empower a nation.

Mrs Edna Mukurazhizha is one of the most dynamic and visionary female leaders in Zimbabwe today. She has been in the financial sector for 20 years. She succinctly describes her rapid career journey in these words: "I started my career as a graduate trainee and I climbed up the corporate ladder to Managing Director of one of the financial institutions in Zimbabwe before I turned 40."

Starting with ZB Bank in 1998 as a graduate trainee, she moved to African Banking Corporation in 2001 as an Account Relationship Manager. In 2004, she moved to Zimbabwe Allied Banking Group (ZABG) to set up Asset Finance. She quickly climbed the managerial ladder and became one of the General Managers of the bank. She left ZABG in 2010 for a top position in BancABC (a regional bank represented in five countries in Africa) in order to set up and manage the bank's Asset Finance Department. During her tenure at BancABC, she had the largest market share. As Country Head Asset Finance, Mrs Mukurazhizha represented BancABC at National Association of Secondary School Heads, i.e. all the government and mission schools in Zimbabwe for two years. In 2015, she was confirmed as Managing Director for BancEASY, a subsidiary for BancABC. She became Managing Director of WEDB Financial Services after she left BancEASY. She is also the founder and current CEO of Empowered Woman Excel Savings and Credit Cooperative – a company she formed in 2020.

She is generally admired and respected within the financial sector for her professionalism, enthusiasm and ability to achieve results, and this has brought her many awards including the following:

Megafest Award: Zimbabwe Top Outstanding Leader of the Year – November 2014.

ZNCC Winner – Banking and Finance Category of the Women in Enterprise Award 2017.

Zimbabwe Business Award: Woman of the Year – Financial Services Industry November 2017.

Women's Business Leadership Award: Top Female Business Leader of the Year March 2018.

Mrs Edna Mukurazhizha's academic background is also impressive. She holds a master's degree in Business Administration (Graduate School of Management), BSc Honours in Economics (University of Zimbabwe), Bank Credit Management Diploma (Damelin School of Management), and Management Leadership Development Programme (University of Stellenbosch). She also serves on a number of not-for-profit organisations and academic committees, including the United Nations Women Leadership Network Zimbabwe steering committee, and the committee for Great Zimbabwe University. She has also written two books: 'You have all it takes Woman Excel' to inspire and empower women not to remain at the same level but excel in every area of their lives. 'In his presence' is a book that supports her faith in Jesus and the miracles she has experienced in her career and private life.

Mrs Mukurazhizha is a strong believer in women empowerment. She expresses her commitment and aspirations in the following words:

> My dream or desire is to have a legacy of having contributed through financial inclusion and women empowerment by increasing the percentage of women with access to capital starting in Zimbabwe and then the world.

Throughout her career, she has encouraged and supported many women to pursue education that will enable them to excel in every area of their lives. In her view, the exclusion of women from the financial sector has generated high levels of poverty and inequality world over. One of her ambitions in life is, therefore, to help women achieve financial independence in order for them to live their lives with purpose and meaning. She seeks to achieve this by motivating women to establish jointly owned and democratically controlled enterprises that will help them fulfil their socio-economic goals. This will also enable the women to invest in the future of their children. The formation of Empowered Woman Excel – the women's Savings and Credit Cooperative Society – in 2020 has been motivated by her passion and commitment to women empowerment. The aim of the credit society is to improve the lives of the members through mobilisation of savings and providing affordable credit as well as investment in real estate. Her thinking is that investments in real estates will enable the women to have stable income through the rentals.

Mrs Mukurazhizha is always focused. Her life is guided by the following 10 principles:

1. Never be content with where you are. Keep developing yourself.
2. Believe in yourself. You were created to excel in every area of your life.
3. Relationships. Life is all about relationships! Pursue peace with all men. Relational capital will take you far.
4. Live healthy. You owe it to your family...Your Health is your Wealth ...Live a balanced life. We are Spirit, Soul and Body.
5. Have an attitude of gratitude. Life is about choices! You are the sum total of the decisions you have made.
6. Never Give up...the area of your greatest pain is the area of your calling.
7. As a man thinks so are you... Whatever the mind can conceive, if you believe you can do it.
8. As a World changer, you need multiple streams of income.
9. Life is about choices and decisions we make; success is not a calling but a decision!
10. Stop complaining! Government is not the answer for the moment. You are the driver of your own destiny.

These principles also guide her work as a philanthropist and a mentor. She has recently started a scholarship programme that offers financial support to students from disadvantaged families, believing that, with a little support and encouragement, some of them will emerge as world changers in their own lives. One of these women is Irene Nyanyiwa who writes the following about Mrs Mukurazhizha's mentorship and support:

> Mrs Mukurazhizha encouraged me to develop myself academically and through these efforts, I have received a degree as well as a driver's licence... I did not have the means at that moment as I had the responsibility of sending my siblings to school, but at the back of my mind, I knew that I had to do it. She helped me to be confident and express myself freely. I always used to feel sorry for myself and that affected my self-esteem. I have had the opportunity to meet and network with influential women through Mrs Mukurazhizha. Her help

as well as help by other women I came to know through her, also enabled me to become passionate about empowering other women and to give them hope.

The Story of Wendy Luhabe – An Outstanding South African Social Entrepreneur[5]

Wendy Luhabe is a South African businesswoman, social entrepreneur and author. She has served as board chair for several organisations, including Vodacom and the Industrial Development Corporation (IDC). She previously worked for 10 years with Vanda Cosmetics and the BMW Group. In 1991, Luhabe founded Bridging the Gap, her first exercise in social entrepreneurship. In 1994, she pioneered the founding of Women Investment Portfolio Holdings, which listed on the Johannesburg Stock Exchange in 1999. From September 2006, she became the Chairperson of the International Marketing Council of South Africa and a Board Member of the Johannesburg Securities Exchange as well as the global business school IMD. She is also the Chancellor of the University of Johannesburg.

A decade ago, she was recognised as one of the top 50 women entrepreneurs in the world by the US-based Star Group and has had three honorary doctorates bestowed on her. In 1997, the World Economic Forum in Davos recognised Luhabe as a Global Leader of Tomorrow. These are certainly laudable accomplishments. However, she approaches life with humility as her remarks below indicate: "While it is wonderful to be recognised for what I have done, I don't attach much value to this and I wouldn't feel less accomplished or do less without it," explains Luhabe. "I think the value in it is that it inspires others to achieve because they can see what is possible. For that I am grateful, because I want women to be inspired to make things happen for themselves."

From humble beginnings in the "old Benoni location" on Gauteng's East Rand, Luhabe says she grew up in a happy home, unaware of the apartheid system. She reflects on her childhood days in the following words:

> Growing up, we didn't know of dreams and ambitions or even how to spell these words – we weren't exposed to an education system that

---

[5] This profile is based on reports and information from multiple Internet sources.

inspired that... We were preoccupied with getting an education and getting food to sustain us.

During her school holidays, Luhabe would assist her grandmother by cleaning homes for people. "Those families would give me their daughters' old clothes as payment," she recollects. Despite her circumstances, her mother – a single parent and a nursing sister – was determined her five children would get an education. She understood the value of education, and she was going to make it a reality for them somehow.

Education in South Africa during the 1960s and 1970s was not a systemic well-directed process. Black women who went to university studied social work, nursing or teaching – their choices were very limited. Consequently, Luhabe started a degree in social work – not because it was something she particularly wanted to do. Her studies were disrupted by the 1976 uprising and she moved to the University of Lesotho, where she began a commerce degree simply because the university did not have any programme in social sciences. She explains: "I didn't have plans to go into business. I didn't know anyone in business. I just planned to get an education to enable me to have a better life."

Despite that, she was one of the first black South African women qualifying with a B.Com degree. She was also the only black woman in the Management Advancement Programme she did at Wits Business School in the mid-1980s. Partly because of being one of the first women with top business qualifications, Luhabe discovered when looking for work that the only jobs available to black women with her qualification were clerical, and she was not going to accept that. "I spent a year searching for a job that would be an opportunity aligned to my qualifications," she says.

"I was eventually introduced to Johan Rupert (South African business tycoon), who offered me a job at Vanda, his cosmetics company." Luhabe has maintained her relationship with Rupert, and was at his 60th birthday in 2010. She is also the chairperson on the board of his company, Vendome SA. She excelled in marketing while at Vanda. "I was comfortable and confident in this area and I thought that this was what I should be doing," she says.

However, after she had motivated and arranged for the designing of skincare products for black women, the company informed her they did not believe there was enough market for the product. Luhabe saw this as a sign that it was time to move on. A year earlier, she had been sitting opposite Eberhard von Koerber, the managing director of BMW, at a breakfast event. "We chatted through the morning and, before it was over, he offered me a job. I didn't pursue it until a year later, when he totally kept his commitment to me." Today, Luhabe is a member of The Club of Rome, a global network (think tank) of leading political, business and science personalities. Von Koerber is the co-president.

Luhabe refuses to engage with the world in her career as a black woman. She explains her views as follows: "I chose to engage as a human being and while I certainly don't disown being a black woman. I just haven't. I wanted to take on the liabilities of engaging as such." Her years at BMW culminated in spending three years working in Germany and the United States. On her return, she was overlooked for a promotion. She viewed the incident as a sign for her to start her own human resources business, a venture she had been thinking about it since the 1980s.

From the beginning of her career, Luhabe got involved with initiatives looking into gender equality in business and the situation of women in the workplace. "It has always been a part of my life," she says.

Her first business, Bridging the Gap, focused on organisational development and training of young graduates and students. "The idea was to help students make informed decisions about what they study and to be better prepared for looking for work," she explains. Like everything she has done, this work was innovative and far ahead of its time.

"I have been blessed to be able to do innovative things. I generally tend to look at what's missing and contribute in areas that are not being addressed," she explains.

Within a year or two, she was involved in discussions on the future of the South African business landscape as democracy was dawning.

I realised then that there were insufficient numbers of women in this picture. The choice was either women wait to be invited into the newly formed organisations or we create our own that will assist pioneering the involvement of women in the economy.

She invited a group of women, including Gloria Serobe, Nomhle Canca and Louisa Mojela, to discuss this, thinking whoever showed up would be involved in the set-up. After 18 months of meeting every Tuesday at 5 p.m. and doing extensive consulting, they came up with a formal model that became Women's Investment Portfolio Holdings (Wiphold). This incredible innovation was a landmark initiative in women's empowerment specifically, and black economic empowerment in general. She says:

> Our idea was to educate women about how the economy works and help them to become first-time investors in a portfolio of businesses we had acquired. This was a real way for women to become shareholders in the economy. So, we became a proxy for a stock market, but in a safe way.

Through Wiphold, they got more than 18, 000 women investing in the economy and they got 300% return on their investment in the first 10 years. They created a trust, which is now worth more than R1 billion.

In 1996, Luhabe wrote a book titled "Defining Moments" (which is also the name of her present company); the book is based on inspiring stories of South African women who have excelled. Hear her:

> I didn't write it because there was an author in me screaming to emerge, I just wanted those stories to be captured so that other women could learn that all life experience has a purpose and it defines us. When we engage with our experiences, particularly the challenging ones, they can enrich our lives.

The proceeds of her book are used to pay for the education of women who are deprived of it through a lack of resources. "I am simply responding to a need as I get so many requests for financial help," stated Luhabe. She doesn't ask for feedback and mostly she doesn't get it. She reveals: "I don't keep records of whom I have helped. I don't do it for that. I have been blessed to be able to change people's lives."

Changing and improving people's lives is something that Luhabe has in common with her husband. "Our professions had nothing to do with bringing us together, we simply fell in love and we both recognised in each other that someone with whom we could share our lives." Some have said that when they met, Shilowa was a bit rough around the edges, but that didn't last long.

"I take no credit for what he has done. When you are with someone, I suppose you inspire each other without actively realising it." Discussing her private life is not something Luhabe finds easy, nor something she was prepared to dwell on. What interests her most is to talk about mentoring and guiding young women:

> The greatest disappointment in our democracy has been what has happened to education. So, my advice to women is make sure you get a good education, as it increases your options in life. It allows you to make independent choices, realise your potential and, when the situation is not right, to walk away. But don't just get the education, use it wisely. Don't waste your talent.

Evidently, Luhabe's higher purpose in life is to help build gender equality in the South African economy. In her view, she has been able to push boundaries beyond what she thought possible because of one key trait – courageous leadership.

> Part of why I've achieved what I have achieved is because I took many risks in my life," she told the delegates at an event in 2017. "I would say courage has possibly been critical to my success. I believe that courage enabled me to take on responsibilities that were way beyond my age and possibly experience. As a result, this positioned me for leadership roles early in my life, in a variety of large institutions. Courage is very much related to one's self esteem, sense of worth, self-belief and overall attitude towards life in general. If all of these are healthy, we are likely to find enough courage to stretch ourselves beyond our comfort zone, she says.

She also attributes her achievement to the direct and indirect mentorship she received from a wide range of people during the formative stages of her life. She recalls: "I was shaped by many people, primarily my mother," while "an early unplanned pregnancy at the age of seventeen taught me much too early about the principles of responsibility and the consequences of our actions.

"My mother was ahead of her time. She was courageous and visionary in her own limited way. She did not let circumstances get in the way of her plans for her life. To witness such rare qualities at a tender age was an inspiration second to none," enthuses Luhabe, with obvious pride.

She reveals further:

> I had amazing teachers who were truly inspirational, among them Matthew Goniwe, anti-apartheid activist and member of the doomed 'Cradock Four' who were assassinated by apartheid police in 1985. He was the best maths teacher I ever came across. I was exposed to political debates at a very young age as I was growing up in Cradock, from people like Rex Luphondwana and Charles Nqakula, former Minister for Safety & Security and later Minister of Defence, who shaped my political consciousness and helped me to understand the brutality of the apartheid system.

She continues:

> At every stage of my professional life and my business life I have been blessed with people who have either opened doors, given me opportunities, mentored me, encouraged me, or believed in me." She states further: "In business, people like Geoff Snelgar, who literally held our hands as we were establishing Wiphold; Leonard Fine, the godfather of private equity in South Africa, who introduced me to his world and taught me about an industry I came to know well enough to enable me to pioneer my own fund for women-owned enterprises. I surround myself with people who know more than I do, who are both interesting and challenging. I only work with people and pursue opportunities where I can both learn and contribute. I ask questions when I do not understand something and I have developed exceptional perceptive and listening skills over the years which have enabled me to respond to challenging situations.

As with all great custodians of ethics, veracity and honour, Luhabe has a strong sense of self and a belief in her fundamental value as a leader. She states:

> I value my ability to think out of the box; to do extraordinary things that make an impact upon society; my commitment to make a difference to the lives of others; my commitment to share my experience to enrich the dreams of those who come behind me; my capacity to touch people's lives; the ability to honour my work and commitments; my ability to shape society and young minds; the courage to question, challenge and take a stand – sometimes alone; the courage to say 'No'; my capacity to enjoy life; my curiosity about the world; my ability to give permission to people to blossom. That is what I value most about myself.

Reflections on the Profiles

Our aim in this book is to give some practical guidelines to those who already have businesses or are contemplating establishing businesses in Africa. We believe that if readers follow these guidelines, their chances of being successful will be greatly enhanced over time. The stories of Messrs. Peter Cunningham, Thatayaone Dichaba, Collen Msasanure, Davidson Norupiri, Chenjerai Tsuro as well as Mrs Edna Mukurazhizha and Ms. Wendy Luhabe provide good evidence of the usefulness of these guidelines.

They inform us about how important it is for entrepreneurs to assess their personal capabilities before plunging into business. Entering business out of necessity does not ensure success. They also underscore the importance of making realistic assessments of the demands that the entrepreneurial role will make on people and their families and the usefulness of cultivating the support of the family in business endeavours. These assessments help entrepreneurs to keep their business perspectives in a sharper focus and guide them as to what they need to do from the outset in order to succeed.

We have argued further that the entrepreneur's mindset is the first key to their success. It is often said that entrepreneurs are driven by an immense desire to achieve the goals they initially set for themselves and then to aim for even more challenging standards. The competitive needs of growth-minded entrepreneurs are to outperform their own previous best results, rather than just to outperform another person. In other words, it is useful to be action-oriented. Successful entrepreneurs are described more as "doers" rather than "dreamers". They are action-oriented people; they want to start producing results immediately. The number or severity of the problems they encounter does not intimidate them. In fact, their self-confidence and general optimism seem to translate into a view that nothing is impossible in business – goals may sometimes just take a little longer. They will work with a stubborn tenacity to solve difficult problems.

Unlike most people, entrepreneurs do not allow themselves to be concerned with failure. They do not think so much about what they are going to do if they do not make it. They rather focus their thoughts and energy on what they have to do to succeed.

The starting point is the determination within us to nurture our potentials and to bring about a real change. When the determination is there, everything else begins to move in the direction that we desire. The moment we resolve to be an achiever, every nerve and fibre within our body immediately orients itself towards our success. It has also been suggested that entrepreneurs should not aim at making money merely for the sake of being rich. They must make profits for a purpose. If you agree with the view that the primary determinant of meaning in life is other people, then you must see your business goals as being closely linked with a desire to create value and make life meaningful for yourself and other Africans and beyond. With such a focus, business owners will develop an inner motivation and tenacity to weather the storms of building viable businesses and designing winning strategies.

A winning strategy requires business owners to pay careful attention equally to both efficiency and effectiveness in their business activities. They will also be willing to develop trust with their business partners as well as other stakeholders in their business circles. A winning strategy also entails managing employees well and choosing the appropriate leadership style. To do this effectively, business owners and their managers must communicate with maturity, engage in fast learning, generate positive human energy, and manage their time effectively. Finally, they must always remember to put their customers at the centre of their decisions. They must see their customers as members of a royal family, i.e. as kings, queens, princes and princesses. Customers are the true employers – even of any business owner. It is because of customers that businesses exist. If any key customer defects to a competitor, s/he leaves with a chain of others; if s/he remains, s/he brings in a chain of other customers.

Business owners and managers are also advised to treat employees as if they are customers. In fact, employees are the main marketing service providers in every business. If they are satisfied, they will be committed to the company and will want the business to succeed, because their own success depends on the success of the business.

Managers must never use threats when dealing with employees. Use of threats will make employees feel displeased and uncommitted and can even turn them against the business. This does not mean that managers should not make them (employees) aware of the negative consequences of not getting the results they (managers) want in the company. It rather means that they (managers) must communicate their expectations in a positive and inspiring manner. Setting inspiring expectations is the most certain way of creating eager and productive employees. However, managers must be specific in their communication. If they want specific results, they must give specific instructions. People work better when they know exactly what is expected of them. It also means that if any of their employees is doing something wrong, s/he should be told. Most people want to improve and will make an effort once they know how to do it.

It is also important to remember that all human beings can be motivated by appealing to their selfish nature. If managers give their employees the opportunity to earn more personally, they will earn more for the company as well.

Furthermore, managers must also make a point of duty to acknowledge the achievements of their employees within the company and in their personal lives. This will make them feel that their managers are paying attention and see them as individuals and not just "human resources". All people like to see that their efforts are not being ignored.

Empowerment is an important source of motivation. Managers must, therefore, allow their key employees to make decisions in matters in which they have professional expertise. We advise that managers must focus on results and not micro-manage every action taken in their companies. This means they must treat mistakes and failures as temporary setbacks on the way to accomplishing their goals. Unlike most people, the bruises of the defeats of growth-oriented business people heal quickly. They have the ability to come to terms with their mistakes, learn from them, correct them, and use them to prevent their recurrence. This allows them to return to the business world again soon after their failure.

One of the major weaknesses of small businesses in Africa is that their owners appear to lack financial discipline. What makes businesses grow is not so much how much their owners earn but how much of their earnings they save and plough back into the company. Therefore, business owners should keep their business accounts separate from their personal accounts. They must determine how much they will have as salaries and maintain a modest lifestyle while their businesses are growing.

Financial discipline will also enable them to get financial support from banks and other financial institutions. When business owners have personal balance sheets and budgets, the information will provide potential lenders with a view of their overall financial situation so they can assess the risk they will be assuming.

As a closing remark, business owners should remember that people see things the way their minds have instructed their eyes to see them. Thus, the first challenge in growing a business is for entrepreneurs to change their mindsets. They must look far ahead into the future – not two years but two or three decades. They must see their businesses growing beyond their own lifetime. With such a long-term orientation, they will see any failure they might experience as just temporary and continue to fight on.

Part 3
Cases

Farmer Business (Pty) Ltd

Farmer Business is located in a suburb of Gaborone, the capital of Botswana. In the mid-2000s, it was established as a broiler farm specialising in production and processing of dressed chickens, chicken portions and by-products. The main inspiration for the establishment of the poultry enterprise was the director who had a degree in agriculture. Farmer Business start-up of a 500-chicken unit was financed from personal funds. However, early in the business, it received a grant of US$5, 156 from the Government financial assistance programme. Initially, Farmer Business was located on a 4, 200-square metre farm plot, which was purchased for US$4, 902. It had its own abattoir and cold storage facilities and was able to stock a maximum of 20, 000 chickens. Later, the company was allocated additional land by Government through the land board. It now has approximately three hectares for relocation of the abattoir due to the closeness of the abattoir to the production units and horticulture production.

The mission of Farmer Business was to be an alternative supplier of chicken portions and by-products by making them accessible and customised. Since its inception, directors/shareholders and management were family members. The main clients of the company were schools, government institutions, restaurants, lodges and individuals. The business had 24 employees (including the two directors).

The annual sales in the 2014 financial year was US$200, 952. However, sales declined by 14% to 172, 923 in the 2015 financial year. The gross profit margin was stable at 24.5% in 2014 and 26% in 2015. The net profit margin dropped from -0.5% to -3% over the period. The company experienced losses of US$1, 023 in the 2014 financial year and US$5, 288 in the 2015 financial year. It operated at -37% below the break-even point in the 2014 financial year and improved to -13% in the 2015 financial year. The challenges faced by the business included low market penetration, low prices for products, losses due to lack of a generator to supply power during power outages, and bio-security breach due to the closeness of the abattoir to the production units.

Although there was 14% decline in sales in 2015, the company was able to trim some of its costs. For example, there was a cut of 21% in cost of sales, 24% in wages, salaries and directors' remunerations and 20% reduction in operating expenses. However, average debt collection period increased from 35 days to 60 days over the period. The average supplier payment period declined slightly from 106 days to 102 over the period. Inventory stood at US$30, 470 and US$29, 068 at the close of the 2014 financial year and the 2015 financial year respectively. The net working capital stood at US$13, 193 and US$23, 533 at the close of the 2014 financial year and the 2015 financial year respectively. This indicates that Farmer Business had funds to satisfy both maturing short-term debts and upcoming operational expenses. The current ratio increased from 1.3 in the 2014 financial year to 1.6 in the 2015 financial year, indicating that the Farmer Business's ability to meet its current obligations had improved (the desired figure is 2). The acid test ratio improved from 0.7 in the 2014 financial year to 0.9 in the 2015 financial year. This indicates that Farmer Business's state of solvency had improved (1 is a healthy level). Although there was an indication that the liquidity had improved, it should be noted that the high accounts receivable accompanied by the length of collection period had a negative impact on this ratio. The company's debt/equity ratio had improved from 7.0 to 1.0 over the period. This had indicated an improvement in Farmer Business's ability to source external finance, bank loans, etc. However, it should be noted that this improvement was mainly due to the conversion of shareholders loans to share capital. The net worth remained positive and increased from US$16, 425 to US$82, 877 over the period.

There was a need to recapitalise Farmer Business, which had not been done since June 2015. This implied that they had to put together a turnaround plan. Farmer Business had the ability to source external finance, bank loans, etc. with its current asset base supported by a sound business and marketing plan. The company had the potential to scale up with appropriate interventions. The diagnostic exercise revealed five broad areas that required interventions. These were strategic management, marketing, sales, production, operations, finance, and quality management. A consultant's report also suggested that the company should develop market segmentation and targeting. Further detailed survey of the market to determine where Farmer Business had a competitive advantage had to be undertaken. It was necessary to implement appropriate marketing and sales plan for each target. For each segment, it was important to develop competitive and profitable product pricing and appropriate communication strategy. It was imperative to train the existing sales force needed in order to generate new business. It was also considered necessary to upgrade the accounting system incorporating cost accounting and monthly management reporting to monitor expenditures and income. Furthermore, working capital was to be increased and cash flow management, including budgeting, was to be improved.

Case Study Questions:

1. Review the entrepreneurial problems that Farmer Business is currently experiencing and discuss the possible reasons for these problems.

2. Advise Farmer Business on how these problems can be addressed to ensure sustainable performance.

Waste Management Pro (Pty) Ltd

Waste management Pro was established in 2010 in Gaborone the capital city of Botswana with a vision to be the champions in the waste management industry, handling hazardous and non-hazardous waste, for both private and corporate clients. Its initial business was to collect and dispose domestic and non-hazardous waste. It later ventured into renting out portable toilets and skip hire for collection of industrial waste and plans to expand into collecting and disposing hazardous and clinical waste as well as waste recycling. The company's warehouse was located in a nearby village and had a branch office in the Northern City. Its main customers were government, the retail sector and individuals.

In 2013, its turnover was US$294, 117 (from US$127, 451 in 2011). Sales increased between 2011 and 2012 by 81%. During the same period, operating expenses rose by nearly 135% (wages alone increased by 93%), resulting in a negative operating income of US$15, 704. Positive developments turned the situation around and the company recorded a net income of US$84, 402 in 2013. The rate of asset utilisation was 1.38 and asset turnover in 2012 was at 1.62. In 2014, the company run into serious financial difficulties; cash and cash equivalents only amounted to only US$254. As such, the company was unable to meet its debt obligations. The acid test ratios of 0.05 in 2014 and 1.13 in 2015 also reflect the dire financial situation. The company had an increased debt to equity ratio in 2015 at 5.32 from -3.91 in 2014, due to an increase in bank loans of US$68, 137 in 2014 needed to finance additional assets and operations. It was important to note that for the period in 2012, there was a halt in business as the owner was away on a short course.

Management considers the company to be in the growth stage and attributes its financial instability to this. The company's assessment revealed six areas that require management attention in order to turn the current financial situation around. These were in strategic management; marketing and sales; production and operations; environmental management; finance; and quality management. Paying attention to these core management activities will enable the company to align its management and operations systems to its objectives.

Case Study Questions:

1. What are the entrepreneurial problems that Waste management Pro's current situation reflects?
2. Advise Waste management Pro on how to address these problems.

Botho Country Lodge (BCL) (Pty) Ltd

Botho Country Lodge (BCL) was founded in the late 1990s as a family business – owned by a husband and wife. It was located in the northern part of Botswana on a 16, 000-square metre plot. Its mission is to provide comfortable accommodation at reasonable prices while meeting the Botswana National Tourism Organisation standards. BCL had humble beginnings, starting as conversion of a family house into a five-room guesthouse. It then gained a lodge status a year after its commencement. Within a number of years, it grew into a 16-room lodge with conference facilities, a pool and bar. The building developments were financed mainly through ploughing back part of the company's earnings, supplemented with the owners' savings and a bank loan of US$320 513.

BCL's main client was the Government, accounting for 90% of the revenue. The remaining 10% was made up of tourists and non-touring individuals. Its official website was www.bcl.lodge.com. It had 18 permanent employees and one internship staff. There were six temporary employees serving in 2015, whereas there were none the previous year. BCL turnover in 2015 was at US$186, 591 and US$130, 101 in 2014. Sales had increased by 43% between 2014 and 2015, i.e. from US$130, 101 in 2014 to US$186, 591 in 2015. The gross profit margin in 2014 was at 64%. This improved in 2015 to 68%. Wages remained almost stable at US$18 615 in 2014 and US$20, 727 in 2015. In 2015, the company took a loan of US$29, 921 to finance further developments on the property. The managing director had indicated that they faced a few challenges vis-à-vis the loan repayments. There are indications that the company's assets were underutilised. Capacity utilisation stood at the rates of 0.29 in 2014 and 0.33 in 2015.

Analyses of 2014 and 2015 figures also reflect increase in productivity, with each employee contributing US$3, 941 to earnings in 2015 compared to US$2, 816 in 2014. Focusing on the net worth over the two-year period, the BCL's net worth slightly increased from US$172, 815 in 2014 to US$188, 263 in 2015. As regards solvency, the current ratio was at 3.16 in 2015, a 29.5% increase from 2.44 in 2014. Inventory accounted for US$7, 986 in 2015 current assets value compared to US$2, 173 in 2014. The acid test ratios were at 2.20 in 2014 and 2.30 in 2015. The company was carrying debts of US$19, 820 in 2015.

There was an inventory conversion period of 33 days in 2015, a decline from the previous year at 13 days. Focusing on gearing, i.e. long-term debt to equity, BCL had a debt-to-equity ratio of 1.77 in 2014 and 2.13 in 2015, reflecting the bank loan obtained for expansion. BCL had an outstanding loan of US$384, 392 with banks. With an interest cover of 1.66 in 2015, the business was able to cover interest commitments to the lenders. BCL assets were predominantly buildings and fittings. These stood at a value of US$559, 078 in 2015.

As noted earlier, 90% of BCL's revenue come from Government orders. This represented some level of risk. The risk arises from the fact that the Government practises supplier rotation. The BCL managing director intimated that there had been a drastic drop in business from the Ministry of Education alone. This was from an average annual sale of US$39, 216 to nearly US$2, 941 only. Although BCL was operating at a healthy gross profit margin of an average of 66%, the operating cost was considered very high. Being situated in the northern tourist part of the country, BCL had the potential for attracting a greater number of customers. However, this potential appeared not to be fully utilised. The managing director attributed this partly to the company having limited skilled management capacity. One manager runs the entire facility. He was not only involved in operational activities but was also engaged in overseeing business development activities. These included the construction of additional structures on the property and the nightclub. The extent to which BCL was involved with the nightclub was not determined. This challenge was compounded by the lack of adequate cash levels and the need to upskill current staff capabilities. The occupancy levels were about 60 % on average. The conference centre brought in the highest portion of revenues.

Management agreed that there was a need to optimise their strengths and abilities in order to manage the business more efficiently. They also needed to focus on improving internal procedures and business practices, and incorporate automation and technology in the business. In the face of a low cash position, they needed to adopt more proactive and strategically targeted sales and marketing meant to not only add to cash but also ensure the facilities are more utilised.

The consultant's assessment revealed eight areas that required attention. These were in strategic management; marketing and sales;

production and operations; finance; human resources; information management; quality management; and technological innovation. Specifically, the areas that required critical intervention were defining the company's mission and vision, and the setting up of strategic objectives. There was also the need for strengthening internal financial administration systems, the analyses of financial information including costing and pricing, the establishment of personnel policies to guide employment issues, strategic collection and use of information, the documentation of procedures to support internal quality standards, and the establishment of a sales management system.

Furthermore, it was agreed that management needed to focus its efforts on consolidating and formalising operations. To support and guide this process, management required to commit skilled management and human resources, and set overall business objectives and action plans (particularly marketing and sales) tied to a business plan to guide the business. Key elements such as increasing revenues and controlling costs also required attention. It was emphasised that it was critical for BCL to enhance and strengthen the management team (which is primarily the ownership), playing off strengths and upskilling where gaps were identified. Systems needed to be put in place which included the constant review of accounting records until the business becomes profitable.

Case Study Questions:

1. What are the entrepreneurial problems that BCL experienced as a business?
2. Advise BCL on what it needs to do or entrepreneurial lessons needed to solve the existing entrepreneurial problems.

ProductionPro (Pty) Ltd[6]

ProductionPro started operations in the Northern City in Botswana, engaged in the supply of protective clothing, embroidery, manufacture and repairs of various tarpaulins and refurbishing of motor vehicle seats and interiors (trimmings). The products are to be sold to a diversity of customers and varying industry sectors in and out of the country. However, its main clients were the railways and utilities companies, meat processing companies and Government departments. The public also formed a part of the clientele. Most of the raw materials utilised for production were imported, mainly from South Africa. The company also has sole (exclusive) dealership in the country for BEIER footwear by a neighbouring country's manufacturer of safety footwear. The initial start-up capital of approximately US$117 647 was from personal finances. The owner then acquired loans and overdraft facilities from various banks thereafter.

The analysis of the financial data provided by the company reveals that sales for the 2014 and 2015 financial years were US$464, 367 and US$657, 364 respectively. According to the managing director, approximately 20% of this income was from the bars and bottle stores. ProductionPro established two liquor outlets (bars) at the suburbs in the 2014 and 2015 financial years. The sales revenue increased to 41% during the period. However, the gross profit margins dropped slightly from 42% in the 2014 to 39% in the 2015. While the sales revenue increased by 41% during the period, the operating expenses increased by only 6%. Thus, the net profit margin increased from 5% in the 2014 to 8% in the 2015. The average debt collection period decreased from 45 days to 35 days over the period. Similarly, the average supplier payment period declined slightly from 49 days to 40 over the period; and the current ratio decreased from 2.5 to 2.0, indicating that the company still had the ability to meet creditors' obligations which fall within 12 months.

The acid test ratio had declined from 1.6 in the 2014 financial year to 1.1 in the 2015 financial year. This indicated that the company's state of solvency had decreased. The debt / equity ratio changed from being negative -37 in the 2014 financial year to 4.6 in the 2015 financial year.

[6] The case is based on interviews with the management and selected staff in order to understand the different elements of ProductionPro. Those interviewed included the accounts officer, stock controller, production, sales and quality control manager, as well as the general manager.

The financial indicators suggested that ProductionPro was in the growth stage. There was an increase of 41% in sales during the period with only a 6% increase in operating expenses, indicating improvement in operations. However, the company experienced some serious management challenges including inadequate staff, high labour turnover, difficulties in market penetration and low demand for its products, resulting in a low inventory turnover. Management, therefore, undertook a diagnostic exercise, which revealed six broad areas that required interventions. These were: strategic management; marketing and sales; finance; human resources; information management; and quality management. Improvements in these areas were considered necessary to enable the company become more competitive, improve its market penetration and expand. For example, it was considered crucial to reorganise and train the sales force in order to generate new business. It was also necessary to set up a stringent working capital / cash flow management, including the inventory turnover, and budgeting was necessary. In that regard, upgrading the accounting system and incorporating costs accounting and monthly management reporting to monitor expenditures and income was also deemed necessary.

Case Study Questions:

1. How will you characterise management and operational decisions of Production Pro?
2. What are the main entrepreneurial problems ProductionPro are currently experiencing?
3. Advise ProductionPro on what it needs to do to solve the existing entrepreneurial problems.

Bibliography

Assimeng, M. (1981). *Social structure of Ghana*. Accra: Ghana Publishing Corporation.

Berne, E. (1964). *Games people play: The psychology of human relationships*. New York: Grove Press.

Covey, S. R. (2004) *The 7 habits of highly effective people*. New York: Simon & Schuster.

Covey, S. R., & Merrill, A. R. (1994). *First things first*. New York: Simon & Schuster.

Dweck, C. (2006). *Mindset: The new psychology of success*. New York: Ballantine Books.

Elkington, J. (2004). Enter the triple bottom line. In A. Henriques & J. Richardson (Eds.), *The triple bottom line: Does it all add up?* London: Earthscan Publications. http://kmhassociates.ca/resources/1/Triple%20Bottom%20Line%20a%20history%201961- 2001.pdf.

Fukuyama, F. (1995). *Trust: The social virtues and the creation of prosperity*. NY: A Free Press.

Hart, S., & London, T. (2005). Developing native capability: What multinational corporations can learn from the base of the pyramid. *Stanford Social Innovation Review*, Summer: 28-33.

Hersey, P. (2007). *Management of organizational behavior* (9th ed.). Upper Saddle River.

Johnson, D. W. (1993). *Reaching out* (5th ed.). Boston: Allyn and Bacon.

Kim, W. C., & Mauborgne, R. (2005). *Blue ocean strategy - How to create uncontested market space and make competition irrelevant*. Boston: Harvard Business School Press.

Kotler, P., & Lee, N. (2009). *Up and out of poverty: The social marketing solution*. Upper Saddle River, NJ: Wharton School Publishing.

Kuada, John (2016) Marketing Decisions and Strategies: An International Perspective (London: Adonis & Abbey Publishers Ltd.)

Kuada, J., & Hinson, R. (2014) Service Marketing in Ghana: A Customer Relationship Management Approach (London: Adonis & Abbey Publishers Ltd.)

Lim, S. G., & Lim, J. H. (2013). *The leader, the teacher and you: Leadership through the third generation*. London: Imperial College Press.

Maxwell, J. (2007). *Failing forward: Turning mistakes into stepping stones for success*. Nashville: Thomas Nelson Inc.

McKinsey Global Institute (2010). *Lions on the move: The progress and potential of African economies.* McKinsey Company. http://www.adlevoc apital.com/images/Lions_on_the_Move.pdf Accessed November 15, 2012.

Millman, D. (2007). *How to think like a great graphic designer.* New York: Allworth Press.

Prahalad, C. K. (2005). *The fortune at the bottom of the pyramid: Eradicating poverty through profits.* Upper Saddle River, NJ: Prentice Hall.

Prahalad, C. K., & Hamel, G. (1990). The core competence of corporations. *Harvard Business Review,* 66, 79-91, May/June.

Tesar, G., & Kuada, J. (Eds) (2013) Marketing Management and Strategy: An African Casebook. (London: Routledge).

Index

A

Admission, 52
Afariwaa Group of Companies, 15
African Banking Corporation, 128
Agambire, Roland, 10, 11, 12, 13, 14
Agams Holding Company, 10
Amanea, Alfred, 29
Asare, Robert, 23

B

Banor, James, 23, 24
Blue Ocean, 85, 88
Boston Consulting Group, 34, 35
Botho Country Lodge (BCL) (Pty) Ltd, v, 149
Botswana, vi, 22, 104, 113, 144, 147, 149, 152
Bulawayo, 110, 112, 113, 118

C

Canca, Nomhle, 135
Cash cows, 34
Celebration Church, Bulawayo, 112
Citizen Entrepreneurial Development Authority, 101
Clear Intentions, 32
Club of Rome, 134
Competency, 52
Consistent Action, 32
Covey, Steven, 20, 33, 103, 154
Cunningham, Peter, v, 105, 139
Customer-centrism, 85

D

Daniel, Peter Jakes, 103
Danso Fruit Drinks, 29, 30
Danso, Charles, 29, 30
Davipel Trading, 116, 118
Dichaba, Thatayaone, v, 100, 139

E

Ebenezer Agricultural College, 108
Emotional knowledge, 75
Environmental Development Group, 25

F

Farmer Business (Pty) Ltd, v, 144

G

Gambia, 22
Germany, 124, 134
Ghana, vi, 10, 11, 12, 14, 22, 23, 24, 25, 28, 29, 30, 103, 154
Ghana Craft Company, 23
Ghana Standards Board, 30
Glasgow Caledonian University, 23
Global Leader of Tomorrow, 132
Great Zimbabwe University, 129

H

Hamara, 105, 110
Hamara Group of Companies, 105
Honesty, 51
Hope City project, 12

I

Integrity, 52

J

Johannesburg Securities Exchange, 132
Johnson, David W, 19, 49, 154

K

kinship obligations, 25
Kiyosaki, Robert, 101, 125

L

Luhabe, Wendy, v, 132, 133, 134, 135, 136, 137, 138, 139

M

Mauritius, 23, 103, 124
Maxwell, John, 16, 17, 154
Mindset, 11, 15, 31, 33, 52, 107, 108, 139
Mojela, Louisa, 135
Msasanure, Collen, v, 112, 113, 114, 139
Mukurazhizha, Edna, v, 127, 128, 129, 130, 139
Munroe, Myles, 103
Mutuality, 52

N

National University of Science and Technology, 112
Norupiri, Davidson, v, 116, 119, 139

O

Obama, Barack, 22
Openness, 52

P

Passionate Commitment, 32
ProductionPro (Pty) Ltd, 152

R

Rapport, 51
Red Ocean, 85
Reliability, 52
Respect for Self and Others, 51
Royal Chunks, 119

S

Sales budget, 93

Serobe, Gloria, 135
Simkovits, Harvy, 51
Sincerity, 51
Sondelani, 109
South Africa, vi, 22, 103, 122, 124, 132, 133, 137, 152
Star Group, 132
Swaniker, Fred, 22

T

Transaction Analysis, 68
Traore, Karim, ii
Triple Bottom Line, 20
Tsuro, Chenjerai, v, 121, 122, 123, 124, 125, 126, 139

U

United States, 14, 34, 121, 124, 134
University of Johannesburg, 132
University of Stellenbosch, South Africa, 129

V

Volta Region, 25

W

Waste Management Pro (Pty) Ltd, v, 147
WEDB Financial Services, 128
Women's Investment Portfolio Holdings, 135
World Economic Forum, 132

X

XYZ Pvt Ltd, 121, 122

Z

Zimbabwe, vi, 22, 103, 106, 109, 110, 112, 113, 114, 116, 118, 119, 121, 122, 123, 128, 129

www.ingramcontent.com/pod-product-compliance
Lightning Source LLC
Chambersburg PA
CBHW021601210326
41599CB00010B/540